"Want to unlock new levels of clarity and courage in your life? Read this book. Within its pages, Krissy Nelson does what she does so well—powerfully encourages and equips her readers with the heart of a mentor and friend."

Shae Bynes, founder, Kingdom Driven Entrepreneur;
author, *Grace Over Grind*

"The dark cloud of shame and fear wants to sabotage our ability to see God, others and ourselves through the Creator's purpose. Krissy's authenticity, coupled with truth, will chart a course for you to discover who you are in Him. You can say goodbye to what has held you back!"

Dr. Melodye Hilton, leadership consultant, executive coach,
author, public speaker and pastor

"You will find yourself moving forward into freedom in this amazing book. My friend Krissy Nelson invites you along on her honest journey of shattering strongholds and breaking through to the limitless realm. This valuable resource targets key mindsets that affect your identity and ability to *go* and *do* what you have been called to. There are biblical and practical directives that will move you into the promises that belong to you. I strongly recommend this timely and interactive manual to everyone!"

Janet Mills, co-founder, International Glory Ministries

"With relatable simplicity and profound truths, Krissy Nelson teaches how to tear down mindsets and walls that reinforce negative emotions in your life. *Say Goodbye to What Holds You Back* is an eye-opening journey of discovery that will launch you into your God-given identity and destiny with joy!"

Lorraine Marie Varela, author, *Love in the Face of ISIS*

T0053998

Say Goodbye to What Holds You Back

SHATTER THE WALLS SURROUNDING
YOU AND BELIEVE WHAT GOD
SAYS ABOUT YOU

KRISSY NELSON

Chosen
a division of Baker Publishing Group
Minneapolis, Minnesota

© 2022 by Krissy Nelson

Published by Chosen Books
11400 Hampshire Avenue South
Minneapolis, Minnesota 55438
www.chosenbooks.com

Chosen Books is a division of
Baker Publishing Group, Grand Rapids, Michigan

Printed in the United States of America

Library of Congress Cataloging-in-Publication Data

Names: Nelson, Krissy, author.
Title: Say goodbye to what holds you back : shatter the walls surrounding you and believe what God says about you / Krissy Nelson.
Description: Minneapolis, Minnesota : Chosen Books, a division of Baker Publishing Group, [2022]
Identifiers: LCCN 2022017702 | ISBN 9780800799670 (trade paper) | ISBN 9780800762872 (casebound) | ISBN 9781493438730 (ebook)
Subjects: LCSH: Christian women—Religious life. | Self-actualization (Psychology) in women—Religious aspects—Christianity. | Identity (Psychology)—Religious aspects—Christianity.
Classification: LCC BV4527 .N375 2022 | DDC 248.8/43—dc23/eng/20220610
LC record available at https://lccn.loc.gov/2022017702

Cover design by Studio Gearbox

22 23 24 25 26 27 28   7 6 5 4 3 2 1

To my daughter, Jenessa.
Never second-guess who God says you are.
Your value is not in what you can do,
but in who God made you to be.
Move forward, my darling, keeping your eyes
fixed on Jesus every day of your life.
He is worth it all.

Contents

Contents

Foreword

THERE ARE TWO KINDS OF DOERS in this world: people who think they can do everything and people who think they can never do enough. The people who think they can do everything often throw shade on those who feel they can never do enough, running circles around them as if they are in a race. The people who think they can never do enough watch in amazement and enter into an internal comparison game that prevents them from ever getting out of the starting gate. The "everys" usually wind up burned out and the "nevers" usually wind up depressed. Either that or the everys become bitter because they also enter into the internal comparison game and dupe themselves into thinking they do all the work. A self-perpetuating problem since they themselves started the race.

If only the everys and nevers could learn to work together. But what would the result be? That the everys would encourage the nevers to do more and become everys? Or that the nevers would warn the everys that burnout is imminent and make them fearfully do less until they are nevers? It is impossible for these two groups to balance out or benefit each other because at their core they are both hopelessly flawed lifestyles. Mere coping mechanisms built upon *doing* instead of upon the biblical standard of *being*.

So if we should not belong to either group—those who think they can do everything and those who think they can never do—what group should we belong to? Krissy Nelson has shed light on a third group—which should be the only group—and that is the flock of people who understand we can do *anything*. And anything is vastly different from everything, because it implies we will only be able to accomplish the things God has assigned us to do . . . with success! Krissy even shares an experience where the Holy Spirit whispered to her, *Krissy, God thinks you can do anything*, inspiring readers to believe the same about themselves.

So whether you are an every, a never or something in between, if you find yourself thinking, *I'm overwhelmed, I'm not enough, I'm afraid* or *I'm stuck*, this book is for you. Because the truth is that both camps ask themselves the internal questions Krissy exposes: *What if people don't like it? What if it isn't profitable? What will this mean for my family or business?* . . . and more. The only difference is that one group is mobilized with frenzy by those thoughts and the other is paralyzed. Krissy has made this book interactive so that you confront each question, find out what Jesus says about it, declare that over yourself, then learn to apply it and pray it into reality. Imagine a life where you are no longer overwhelmed or stretched too thin! It's time for you to be free of the war in your head. It's time for you to say goodbye to what holds you back.

Laura Harris Smith, author; TV host,
naturopathic doctor

Introduction

"WHO AM I, LORD?!" I cannot tell you how many times I have asked the Lord this question. Over the years, in each new season of life, this is my recurring question.

It poured from my heart when I was fourteen, in the form of deep sobs and agony. I was unsure God would even answer my plea. But He did. I will share more about that in the pages of this book.

Then, as a young adult entering the work force, then as a new wife, then as a new mom, then branching into a new career, starting over, moving cross-country, as an author, in ministry, and so on. With each turn, the words *Who am I, Lord?* have resurfaced in a brand-new context.

From the time I was fourteen, I have sought the Lord on my identity as I leaped into new territory. What I have learned is this. The answer, though uniquely presented, returns to me the same each and every time: *You are Mine.*

Questioning our identity in Christ is an attack from the enemy. He aims to bog us down in defeat, insecurity, perfectionism and shame so we cannot thrive in who God says we are.

Who are we? We are His revived, beautiful, vibrant daughters. We are full of life and hope and called to live joy-in-Jesus lives. The question is, Why aren't we? Why do we get weighed down by life's challenges? Why do the storms seem to throw us off course? How do we get to the point of feeling that we are in a box, unable to climb out and thrive in who God created us to be?

We need an encounter with our King Jesus in which our hearts are revived all over again and the walls boxing us in crumble to the ground.

This process is the journey. The journey is the process.

Imagine a winding road and you are moving forward, but as you go you encounter one wall after the other. Do you stop at the wall and say, "Well, I guess this is it—I'm not meant to advance any further"? Or do you see that wall as an opportunity to draw on the divine resources you have been given through Christ and watch the wall crumble to the ground?

This book is a clarion call to you, my friend, to let your light shine brightly. To arise in this time to your unique identity in Christ. To rediscover who He says you are so you can experience the vibrant life of joy found in Jesus through every storm, every challenge, in each unique season.

Life has its challenges. As women, we carry a lot of weight on our shoulders. The weight of our own burdens. The weight of our families, friends, work. Even the weight of what we see occurring in the world around us. If we are not careful, we can become empty. Dry. Once-vibrant life grows dull and heavy. Areas in which we have struggled become walls blocking us from thriving in who God created us to be. We become shells of ourselves.

How do we reverse this? How do we return to the joy-filled life in Jesus we experienced when we first met Him? We surrender all over again. We let go and let Jesus revive our tired and weary hearts.

Shame, fear, perfectionism and overthinking are just four of the walls keeping us from thriving in who we are in Christ. Those walls leave us full of fear, as if we are not enough, overwhelmed and just plain stuck.

I would like to journey with you through this book to see these walls shatter to the ground. Together we will emerge as a force, focused fiercely on Jesus, embracing His call fully and believing what God says about us.

Let me be clear—I do not write as an expert, having figured out and mastered this stuff. No, I write to you as a friend, one who is on the journey with you, taking what I have learned (and am learning) so far along the way and sharing what the Lord is showing me. I am hungry to live my life believing what God says about me every step of the way. I need this book as much as the next gal.

So let's journey together, exposing the walls holding us back, and smashing them to the ground with Jesus—revived and thriving in who God says we are.

Jesus is worth the effort, and He is the One who does the heavy lifting. You simply remain on the path, surrender your life, allow Him to do the work in you, and watch what He will do when you refuse to settle for simply surviving the day and truly thrive in who you are in Christ.

I have been on a journey to say goodbye to what holds me back so I can move forward in all that God has for me, thriving in who He says I am. It has not been easy, but the fruit of trusting Him every step of the way is incredible. Trusting God without seeing all the details has been a key for me.

How do we do that when we are faced with wall after wall, making us feel as though we are not enough, or feeling afraid, overwhelmed or just plain stuck?

Well, I will tell you how—with the wrecking ball of truth! Those walls are not meant to hold us back, but to be broken down to the ground. It is time for us to move forward.

In this book you will:

- Identify walls keeping you feeling as though you are not enough, or feeling full of fear, overwhelmed or stuck.
- Rediscover your joy in Jesus so you can believe what God says about you.
- Gain tools for the journey to see those walls shatter to the ground.
- Move from daily survival to daily revival through Jesus.

You are called to shatter the walls and shine brightly for Jesus, not just surviving, but thriving in who God created you to be.

A lie is just a lie until we believe it. Once we believe it, it becomes our own thought. The more we think that thought, we build a mindset. Once the mindset is established, it becomes a wall we hide behind, finding it nearly impossible to move forward.

This book is all about moving forward and watching those walls shatter to the ground as we believe what God says about us. So say goodbye to what holds you back, my friend, and say hello to all that God has for you. We are surging forward with a shout full of joy and victory in Jesus!

How to Read

Each chapter, broken down into five parts, discusses a mindset, a wall and how to move forward:

- Part 1: I'm Not Enough
- Part 2: I'm Afraid

- Part 3: I'm Overwhelmed
- Part 4: I'm Stuck
- Part 5: I'm Free!

You will learn about the mindsets and walls reinforcing the four key negative emotions we face so you can see those walls shatter to the ground and you can move forward in freedom. You can read this book cover to cover or break it up into a five-week study with a group.

In each chapter you will glean from my own experience of each wall, what I have learned and what the Lord is saying to you now. Each chapter ends with four equipping tools to help you shatter the wall and believe what God says about you:

1. Jesus Says
2. Declare It
3. Apply It
4. Prayer

This book is interactive, so grab a fresh journal, a pen or pencil, and a red pen as you prepare to go through these pages.

Friend, I am excited for you to join me in this journey toward believing what God says about you. You are not meant to live less than the life Jesus died for you to live. You are not meant to be trapped behind those walls feeling not enough, afraid, overwhelmed or stuck. You have been divinely chosen by a God who loves you, has a plan for you and believes in you.

So say goodbye to what holds you back, see the walls shatter to the ground and believe what God says about you.

> He who began a good work in you will carry it on to completion until the day of Christ Jesus.
>
> Philippians 1:6

Father, I thank You for the amazing woman reading right now. Encounter her as she soaks in each word. Let Your presence fall afresh on her even now, restoring hope that has been lost and joy that has been stolen. Awaken the dreams of her heart as she experiences a reviving from deep within, seeing these walls come crumbling down. Thank You for her uniqueness, for how You have set her apart and created her truly special. May she thrive daily in who You have created her to be, living the vibrant, joy-in-Jesus life You always intended her to live.

PART 1

I'm Not Enough

Definition of *being enough*

1. Equal to what is needed.
2. Occurring in such quantity, quality or scope as to fully meet demands, needs or expectations.

Mindsets

1. I'll never be good enough.
2. There's something wrong with me.
3. Someone else can do it better.

Walls

1. Shame
2. Insecurity
3. Comparison

1

I'll Never Be
Good Enough

I JUST DON'T FEEL as if I'm enough. Have you ever felt this way—with a nagging sense that who you are and what you have to offer somehow fall short?

Most women can relate to this feeling. But what is it? And why do we feel this way so often?

In many seasons of life, I have felt totally inadequate. In fact, I have come to expect that I will likely always have a sense of inadequacy. Why? Because what God has called me to do is way bigger than me.

It has taken some time, but I have finally learned to reframe that sense of "I don't feel as if I'm enough" from a negative to more of a neutral place. I don't know that I would call it a positive just yet, but I don't give it the weight I once did.

But it has not been an easy mindset to work through, let me tell you. It is convincing. And it offers us a false sense of comfort that we can back out of our commitments for the greater good, because it would just be better to have someone else attend to whatever it is, rather than me . . . because I'm not good enough, right?

I will never forget when I began writing my first book, *Created for the Impossible*. The title alone might cause you to think its author was super bold and had no walls to shatter or mindsets to overcome, right? Well, if you thought this, you would be wrong. I was super thankful to finally be moving forward with God's call on my life to write a book, as it had been seventeen years since He had spoken this assignment over my life, when I was just seventeen. But it was actually through the process of writing that I overcame a lot of troublesome mindsets I did not even realize I was still dealing with.

That is one beautiful thing about what God asks of us. He is not asking us to be perfect before we start; He is looking only at our willingness to move forward and trust Him in the journey. The perfecting comes as we go. As we move forward, He molds and shapes us. He loves working with our simple obedience.

You're not enough, Krissy. Who do you think you are? You should just quit. These words went through my mind each morning as I got up at 4:00 a.m. to write.

I am not going to lie; it was challenging to move forward. I found that I could not argue with the notion of not being enough or not being qualified . . . yet I sensed this was sort of the point. If I were to write a book to help people move from where they are now to where they want to be, and to bring about real transformation, it could not be about my being enough, right? It had to be bigger than that—but I could not quite put my finger on it.

So each day as I showed up to write, I would fight this mindset and pray, "Jesus, give me what I need to accomplish what You're asking of me. Empower me to do what feels impossible."

And each day He did just that. He showed up in beauty and power, speaking into my identity, reminding me that it is His life running through my veins.

As I moved forward in my writing, I began to realize that the mindset of "I'm just not enough" was a form of shame for my inadequacies. I realized the enemy was messing with my mind, making me ashamed of my humanity.

After the Lord told Paul, "My power is made perfect in weakness," Paul said, "I will boast all the more gladly about my weaknesses, so that Christ's power may rest on me" (2 Corinthians 12:9). This is an empowering teaching for those of us who feel shame over our inadequacies. It reminds us that we have built-in gaps, and those gaps are nothing to be ashamed of. Rather, we should rejoice, since those vacancies make room for the power of God to fill us and operate through us.

Day in and day out, as I showed up to write, I felt stronger and stronger. Without realizing it, I was embracing my weaknesses, and God's power was being perfected in and through me. I was doing the impossible because I am created for the impossible—and so are you!

Here is where it all changed. One morning as I moved from the kitchen to the living room, careful not to spill my fresh cup of hot coffee, I was stopped in my tracks as the Holy Spirit spoke a truth right to my soul.

Krissy, He whispered, as if He had a secret to tell me that I needed to stand still for, *God thinks you can do anything.*

It was a statement I had heard from well-known Bible teacher Marilyn Hickey a few years earlier: "God thinks you can do anything." Everything in the room seemed to freeze in real time as God delivered that statement to my heart through Marilyn's words. I did not hear it as a question, as though God were not sure; I heard it as His opinion of me—one of His thoughts that, according to Isaiah 55:9, are higher than our thoughts. I could be all that God has called me to be. Those words revived my heart and set me on a trajectory toward the "more" of God.

Now, as I moved with my morning coffee from the kitchen to the living room, I felt the power and presence of God surround me and pull me in tight.

The Holy Spirit continued, *He knows it.* And He reminded me that "the Spirit of him who raised Jesus from the dead is living in you" (Romans 8:11).

I felt unraveled, as if all the tight winding of my own ambitions and efforts to become "enough" were being recalibrated in that moment. I really got it. It was not about my ability to become something. It was about the vacancies inside me that make room for God to use me as He wills for His plans and purposes on the earth. You can be all He has called you to be.

Tears welled up in my eyes as I said, "Thank You, Jesus. Thank You that I don't have to be enough to be someone or something. Thank You that You are more than enough. Thank You that when I have You, I have everything I need."

Friend, in that moment the wall of shame came shattering to the ground. I was no longer concerned over where I lacked. I rejoiced with God that He desired to use me and *was* using me.

The Wall: Shame

The dictionary defines *shame* as "a painful emotion caused by consciousness of guilt, shortcoming or impropriety." Think about that—a consciousness of our shortcomings; the sense that we are not enough.

How sneaky, right? Shame masquerading as this super common, often overlooked sensation of "I am just not enough."

A recent study found that eight out of ten millennials feel they are not good enough in most areas of their lives as compared to their peers and those in older generations.[1]

The "I'm not enough" mindset comes in many shapes and sizes. Our inner dialogue sounds a lot like this:

• I'll never be good enough.
• Someone else can do it better.
• Who do I think I am?
• Why me?
• I'm not qualified.

This debilitating mindset has the ability to hold us back, overwhelm us and keep us stuck. Many have fallen victim to the wall of shame. I know I have. There is something about that feeling of "I'm not enough" that sends a chill down our spines. If we are not enough, then why do we even bother, you know?

But this mindset is agreeing with a lie—a lie that has us convinced we should give up without even trying. The result: I am ashamed of my accomplishments (or lack thereof) and find that sense of "I'm not enough" washing over me.

Living from this mindset roots us in a false identity, one undeserving of anything good, of anything redemptive, of anything contrary to the overwhelming sense that we just are not good enough for what we hope to become or achieve.

But this thinking is contrary to the Word of God. It is the opposite of what God says about us. Sure, we all fall short. But that is not the point. The point is, our being undeserving is exactly why Christ came to save us. It is because we fall short

1. John Anderer, "Inferiority Complex: 8 In 10 Millennials Believe They Aren't 'Good Enough,'" November 4, 2019, Study Finds, https://www.studyfinds.org /inferiority-complex-8-in-10-millennials-believe-they-arent-good-enough.

that He died. And because of the blood of the Lamb of God, Jesus Christ, shed on the cross two thousand years ago on our behalf, we do not have to live weighed down by the fact that we fall short. Rather, we can live fully alive and grateful for the sacrifice Jesus made to bring us into the abundant life—not because we deserve it but because it is God's redemption plan to bring us back to Himself and draw us near.

Shame says, "I'm not enough."

Jesus says, "I'm more than enough."

The Trap

The enemy wants to trap you to prevent you from moving forward. The dictionary defines the action of *trapping* as "catching or taking in or placing in a restricted position." How can we move forward when we are taken captive or placed in a restricted position? We can't.

This is why 1 Peter 5:8 admonishes us to "be alert and of sober mind. Your enemy the devil prowls around like a roaring lion looking for someone to devour." (We will look at this passage in more detail in chapter 4.) The enemy sets traps for us through these mindsets in hopes that we become permanently disabled, restricted and stuck.

In each chapter of this book, then, I will expose the trap the enemy sets through each mindset, to empower you to move forward and see the restricting walls shatter to the ground.

In the case of the mindset *I'll never be good enough*, the trap is set when we believe we should continue striving to try to measure up. Until then we are paralyzed—convinced we will never be enough and that we should not even bother moving forward.

The enemy wants to keep you in a perpetual state of "I'm not enough" so you never move forward. Often we go about our day-to-day lives so accustomed to how things are that we never expect—or dream of asking for—anything to shift in our lives. Like the woman at the well in Samaria living day to day, with no expectation that circumstances could, should or would be any different than they are right now.

Let's look at her story in the gospel of John. The Samaritan woman is going about her normal routine when she encounters Jesus at the well—the same well she draws from regularly. Jesus is sitting by that well; His disciples have gone into town to buy food.

> Jesus said to her, "Will you give me a drink?" . . . The Samaritan woman said to him, "You are a Jew and I am a Samaritan woman. How can you ask me for a drink?" (For Jews do not associate with Samaritans.)
>
> John 4:7, 9

Let's pause right there. In these verses we see the first signs of "I'm not enough" in the Samaritan woman. She is saying to Jesus, "You're not supposed to be talking to me. You're a Jewish man and I'm a Samaritan woman. This is unheard of." She is aware of her shortcomings.

> Jesus answered her, "If you knew the gift of God and who it is that asks you for a drink, you would have asked him and he would have given you living water."
>
> verse 10

Whoa! Jesus is breaking the rules to reach this woman, and He is saying, "Not only are you important and valuable for Me to stop and speak with you, but I want to give you something. This something is the very thing you desperately need but don't even know to ask for. This something will change your life. This something is a gift from my Father—your Father."

25

She does not understand. The wall of shame is clouding her view and impairing her ability to recognize the gift of God.

> "Sir," the woman said, "you have nothing to draw with and the well is deep. Where can you get this living water? Are you greater than our father Jacob, who gave us the well and drank from it himself, as did also his sons and his livestock?"
>
> verses 11–12

You see, she is still thinking in terms of the natural, the "possible"—all she knows and all she thinks she deserves.

> Jesus answered, "Everyone who drinks this water will be thirsty again, but whoever drinks the water I give them will never thirst. Indeed, the water I give them will become in them a spring of water welling up to eternal life."
>
> verses 13–14

The woman begins to realize how thirsty she really is. It is a deep thirst, a soul thirst she now realizes can be quenched only one way—and she is ready.

> The woman said to him, "Sir, give me this water so that I won't get thirsty and have to keep coming here to draw water."
>
> verse 15

Can you see that wall of shame, the wall of "I'm not enough," beginning to shatter? It happens as we commune with Jesus and encounter Him, and He us, in our day-to-day lives.

During your ordinary, your mundane, your going to the well to draw water—or, in today's culture, filling your mug with coffee from your Keurig in between loads of laundry or on a lunch break at work—Jesus is there. He is right there waiting to have an encounter with you. To talk with you about your day. To offer you what you did not know you needed—a drink of living water, fresh and new today. Will you take Him up on His offer?

Jesus knows exactly what wall she is facing in her life, exactly which mindset she has bought into that hinders her from believing how God sees her, preventing her from a real relationship with Him. Now that He has the conversation going, He confronts the wall head on.

> He told her, "Go, call your husband and come back."
> "I have no husband," she replied.
> Jesus said to her, "You are right when you say you have no husband. The fact is, you have had five husbands, and the man you now have is not your husband. What you have just said is quite true."
>
> verses 16–18

Surprised, she recognizes Him as a prophet. Jesus tells her,

> "A time is coming and has now come when the true worshipers will worship the Father in the Spirit and in truth."
>
> verse 23

Then Jesus reveals to her who He is.

> The woman said, "I know that Messiah" (called Christ) "is coming. When he comes, he will explain everything to us."
> Then Jesus declared, "I, the one speaking to you—I am he."
>
> verses 25–26

Up to now, He has been careful not to reveal Himself prematurely to the Jews, yet He goes ahead and unveils what is coming and who He is to this Samaritan woman. Why would

He do this? Because she needs to see herself in Him. He deposits these seeds of truth into the empty, thirsty places in her heart. And suddenly she knows who she is, too—a daughter, a lost one who has been found.

> Then, leaving her water jar, the woman went back to the town and said to the people, "Come, see a man who told me everything I ever did. Could this be the Messiah?" They came out of the town and made their way toward him.
>
> verses 28–30

This one who was sharply aware of her inadequacies has now found fulfillment through her Messiah. Her thirst is quenched in Jesus and her shame washed away.

She even leaves her water jar at the well—the very vessel she brought to fill with water. Why would she leave it there? The answer is what we are all meant to catch here, my friend. She leaves her vessel at the well because she has received the gift from the Father that Jesus offered her. Life. Living water springing up within her. As she runs from the well, she has become the vessel filled with the life-giving water she received from Jesus.

The wall of shame shatters as she discovers who she is in Christ. He has filled all her inadequacies with His living water, His Holy Spirit. She has been made brand-new in Jesus.

The Wall Shatters

The wall of shame shatters as we allow the truth of what Jesus says about us to take root. You see, Jesus meets us right where we are and says, "I have a drink for you. Where you feel you lack, I am all-sufficient. Where you long for more, I will satisfy."

The goal is not ever for us to feel that we are enough. We are never enough. No, the goal is for us to recognize our need for Jesus. It is only through Him that we feel fully satisfied. We may always be aware of our weaknesses, but let's aim to be like Paul in 2 Corinthians 12:8–10 (as we saw earlier) and say, "You know something? I will boast in my weakness, because that's where God's power is made perfect in me!"

Moving Forward

What happened to the woman at the well? We watch her begin to dig deeper, drawing from His well of truth . . . of life . . . of living water. Jesus' words pour over her, causing that wall of shame to crumble to the ground. He gives her an invitation to know Him—to really know Him.

> "Woman," Jesus replied, "believe me, a time is coming when you will worship the Father neither on this mountain nor in Jerusalem. You Samaritans worship what you do not know; we worship what we do know, for salvation is from the Jews. Yet a time is coming and has now come when the true worshipers will worship the Father in the Spirit and in truth, for they are the kind of worshipers the Father seeks. God is spirit, and his worshipers must worship in the Spirit and in truth."
>
> verses 21–24

She is beginning to see more clearly. She is close . . . she is really close. He has met her right where she is in her life and understanding. She is about to be consumed by truth that will wash over her and surge forth within her—that "spring of water welling up to eternal life" that Jesus described earlier.

This is when she mentions the coming Messiah, and Jesus declares to her, "I, the one speaking to you—I am he" (verse 26).

And that is that. Truth overcomes her and new life rushes through her.

What happens after she runs back to town to announce to all the people that the Messiah has come and that He has living water to offer them all?

> Many of the Samaritans from that town believed in him because of the woman's testimony, "He told me everything I ever did." So when the Samaritans came to him, they urged him to stay with them, and he stayed two days. And because of his words many more became believers.
>
> They said to the woman, "We no longer believe just because of what you said; now we have heard for ourselves, and we know that this man really is the Savior of the world."

verses 39–42

Friend, the woman's wall of shame shattered to the ground when she encountered truth and her soul was satisfied. Her life was completely and utterly transformed when she encountered Christ—when she took her first drink of water from the well that never runs dry. As she ran from that well, as we saw, she left the very thing she had brought with her that needed filling—her water jar. Her life became the water jar, and Jesus' living water satisfied even her natural thirst.

You have access to that same well today, my friend. That well is Jesus. He has living water to offer you today. His love for you will quench your thirst and shatter that wall of shame once and for all—the wall that has been looming in front of you and convincing you that you are not enough.

Jesus offers you that drink today. Will you receive it? Will you reach out your hand and drink from the well that never runs dry, never to thirst again?

Can you hear that wall of shame beginning to shatter? Listen closely and wait on the Lord; you will hear it. Say goodbye to shame, my friend, and continue to move forward believing that, although we are never enough, God's power is made perfect in weakness, and in Jesus we feel fully satisfied.

Believe What God Says about You

He said to me, "My grace is sufficient for you, for my power is made perfect in weakness." Therefore I will boast all the more gladly about my weaknesses, so that Christ's power may rest on me.

2 Corinthians 12:9

Jesus Says: I am more than enough, so through Me, you are more than enough, too.

Declare It: Where I lack, Jesus is all-sufficient. Therefore, I am enough.

Apply It: Receive Jesus' gift of living water and His promise that, in your weakness, His power is made perfect. Trade your shame for the power in His name. You are free! Write down the areas in which you have felt you are not enough. Now take your red pen and write, "Jesus is more than enough."

Prayer

Thank You, Jesus, for demolishing on the cross the power of shame. Help me to believe what You say about me. Shatter the wall of shame to the ground as I embrace Your love, power and joy in my life that I was worth Your dying for. You bring me into the presence of God because He deserves what You died for—me.

2

There's Something Wrong with Me

FOR AS LONG AS I CAN REMEMBER, I have yearned to feel part of something. I wanted to fit somewhere. I longed to find other people who were like me. But the more I searched, the more disappointed I became, because I never really found a large group of people about whom I could say, "I fit here."

I am not exactly sure why God never had a group for me. But as I get older, I can honestly say that my path has been unique. In my teenage years, and even in various seasons in my adult years, this caused me to feel insecure about who I was. *Why don't I fit anywhere?* I would ask the Lord, and later my husband. *There must be something wrong with me.* This was my mindset for many years.

Meanwhile I continued to move forward, wishing and hoping that this elusive group would find me, or I would find it.

In my teens I was thankful to find a few girlfriends with whom I really connected. In fact, I could call them today at any moment and they would drop everything to be there for me, and I for them. (You know who you are.)

Since I married young (a few months before my twentieth birthday), my husband, Donovan, became my "person," and he and I really grew up together. We did not have many friends, and both of us, homebodies that we are, did not feel we needed much more. We were really close with our family, and that was fulfilling. We now have a handful of very close friends and feel extremely blessed.

In my thirties, as I launched out into full-time ministry, the feeling of wanting a group began to surface again. I felt I needed this in order to continue forward in ministry, and I tried to find others like me—who taught as I did, preached as I did, wrote as I did, leaped into new projects, media and motherhood as I did. But a group was not to be found. While I did plug into a variety of groups, I never really fit with any one of them exclusively.

So again, "There must be something wrong with me" surfaced, and insecurity began to settle in. If we allow it to.

Have these words ever crossed your mind?

Let's be real and honest. This statement carries weight. It has the power to derail us, halt us and prevent us from stepping forward into who God says we are—His treasured daughters. And it hinders us from believing what God says about us, as opposed to what we think others are saying or thinking about us. If we allow it to.

I cannot tell you how many times I have entertained this thought and even gone so far as to declare it over myself throughout the years. What starts as a feeling can turn quickly into a declaration that we speak over ourselves, and we go, *Yep. There is something wrong with me.*

Why do we do this?

For as long as I can remember, I have been asking myself the question "Who am I?"

I explained in the last chapter that God had called me to write a book. It was actually through the process of writing that I overcame a lot of troublesome mindsets I did not even realize I was still dealing with.

Then, when I was 26, and Donovan and I had been married for seven years, Grandma Jackie, my father's mother, passed away. It was my first loss of someone close to me.

I will never forget sitting next to her grave, tears spilling from my eyes. Something about her passing had stirred a desire in me to write that book I had long dreamed of writing.

What would I even write about? I asked myself, sitting on a blanket in the middle of the graveyard, staring at my beloved grandmother's name etched on the stone before me. It was as if the answer echoed from some nearby friend: *The search for self.*

It seemed like a mountain I was ill-equipped to scale. Nevertheless I decided to give it a try. What I would write and how I would write it was a mystery. All I knew was, I had to do *something*. For as long as I could remember, this quest had always been at the top of my mind and heart.

One year later came the life-changing day when I learned I was pregnant with our first child—the daughter God would use as part of His answer to the resounding question in my heart and mind: *Who am I?*

We all ask this question at some point. Often we look to the world around us to clarify the answer. But if we are not careful, we will allow the wrong source to provide the answer God never intended we receive. This was me for so many years.

Who am I?

- I'm a worker.
- I'm a manager.
- I'm a wife.

- I'm a friend.
- I'm in the fitness industry.
- I work with people.
- I like spending time with my family at "the lakes" (as people from Minnesota, "land of 10,000 lakes," say).

The list goes on and on. And these are all fine answers. But they weren't *the* answer. The answer I needed would become clear to me only in the years to follow, as I truly lost myself, only to cry out to God from the depths of my soul and hear His answer like a drink of water to my weary soul: *You are Mine.*

You see, the Bible gives away the answer time and time again throughout its pages: "'In him we live and move and have our being'" (Acts 17:28). "Christ in you, the hope of glory" (Colossians 1:27). "To all who believed him and accepted him, he gave the right to become children of God" (John 1:12 NLT). And much more.

We are His and He is ours.

This is where our story starts.

And in Him we discover who we truly are. His daughters. Bought with a price. Born for a purpose. Created for the impossible.

Your life has inestimable value, my friend.

I want you to really hear those words, so I will say them again: Your life has inestimable value. Jesus went to inconceivable lengths to save you, redeem you, wash you and restore you to right standing with the Father. Why? Because you are precious in God's sight. You are a treasure. (Jesus said in Matthew 10:31 we are "worth more than many sparrows.") He loves you so much.

I want you to speak this over yourself right now. Repeat after me, "My life has inestimable value. Jesus loves me so much."

Now pause. What do you feel? Close your eyes right now and say those words again. I will wait.

I don't know about you, but I have tears streaming down my face right now as I am writing these words and speaking them over my own life. The fact that Jesus loves me this much—to declare with His life and death on the cross that I was worth the effort—is astonishing to me. Why? None of us deserves it, do we? Of course not. The Bible says we are all sinners. But then it says, "It is by grace you have been saved, through faith" (Ephesians 2:8).

The dictionary defines *grace* as "unmerited divine assistance given to humans for their regeneration or sanctification." Unmerited—meaning totally undeserved. We did not deserve it, but He offered it to us anyway. Jesus rescued us in our time of greatest need by reconciling us to the Father through His own blood so we could live free and full of life and hope and full of Him, Jesus.

Don't you see—you are a product of God's deep love for you! His love trumps your disbelief. His love triumphs over your sins. His love draws you in, cleans you up and rewrites your destiny. You are His. That is who you are.

Abba Father is speaking this over you now. He is saying, "You are Mine."

His love brings us full circle in life giving us a brand-new start.

"Forget the former things; do not dwell on the past. See, I am doing a new thing! Now it springs up; do you not perceive it? I am making a way in the wilderness and streams in the wasteland."

Isaiah 43:18–19

It is okay to say goodbye to the old things and embrace the new things God is doing. In fact, we are urged to "forget the former things" and gaze upon the new. What a gift!

You are unique, my friend. Not only is there nothing wrong with you, but there is no one else out there quite like you. God is inviting you into the new today and asking you to embrace who He has made you to be once and for all. God thinks you are amazing, beautiful, talented and one of a kind. He should know—He made you that way.

The Wall: Insecurity

The dictionary defines *insecurity* as "being deficient in assurance; beset by fear and anxiety; not confident or sure." Simply put, insecurity is rooted in fear. The fear that there is something wrong with you. The fear of missing out. The fear of not being connected. The fear of getting it wrong and the consequences that follow.

Our inner dialogue sounds a lot like this:

- There must be something wrong with me.
- I'm going to miss out on something.
- I should be more connected than I am.
- Why don't people seem to like me once they get to know me?

Let's look at the story of Peter. His life demonstrates that our journey in discovering who we are in Christ is just that, a journey. We see Peter go from Jesus' initial invitation—"Come, follow me" (Matthew 4:19)—to the book of Acts, when three thousand people were converted to Jesus Christ in one day.

We see his ups and downs along the way. Walking on water, denying Jesus, recognizing Him as the Son of God, and more. But something happened when Peter was questioned about his affiliation with Christ. He denied knowing Him. He denied any association with Jesus whatsoever.

Jesus had been arrested in the Garden of Gethsemane and all His disciples had fled. Later, while Jesus was being interrogated by the high priest, at the beginning of the long night leading to His execution, Peter was hanging around nearby.

> Now Peter was sitting out in the courtyard, and a servant girl came to him. "You also were with Jesus of Galilee," she said.
> But he denied it before them all. "I don't know what you're talking about," he said.
> Then he went out to the gateway, where another servant girl saw him and said to the people there, "This fellow was with Jesus of Nazareth."
> He denied it again, with an oath: "I don't know the man!"
> After a little while, those standing there went up to Peter and said, "Surely you are one of them; your accent gives you away."
> Then he began to call down curses, and he swore to them, "I don't know the man!"
> Immediately a rooster crowed. Then Peter remembered the word Jesus had spoken: "Before the rooster crows, you will disown me three times." And he went outside and wept bitterly.
>
> Matthew 26:69–75

Why did Peter deny knowing Jesus? Why did he fall into this trap of timidity over his identity as a follower of Christ? He had insecurity rooted in the fear of what might happen to him if he acknowledged being a follower of Jesus. Jesus was in the throes of the trial that would lead to His death. Peter was caught up in the noise all around him. Amid all the chatter surrounding who Jesus was, Peter was beginning to question who he was as a result.

Can you imagine—questions and accusations flying all around like bullets? What would happen if Jesus was not who He said He was? What would happen to Peter? These questions brought so much doubt and fear that his first reaction to the questions about his affiliation with Christ was to deny Him.

But there is something much deeper here for us to recognize. This something points to the reality and power of "Christ in us" (as we saw earlier from Colossians 1:27), which happens when we surrender our lives to Him, deny ourselves, take up our crosses and follow Him—the process of becoming a disciple (see Matthew 16:24). Being a follower of Christ had not yet seeped into Peter's heart as the core of his identity, so he was not able to pass the test when questioned about his affiliation with Jesus.

He had spent years following Jesus physically, but had not fully surrendered his heart spiritually as a true disciple. He had not yet taken up his cross, willing to deny himself and forsake all else, if it meant forever following Christ. His identity was not in Jesus . . . not yet. Peter still had a limited view. But his spiritual sight would soon come into full view in the moments and days to follow.

You see, following after Christ with our hearts is what transfigures us into His image and rewires our identities from who we once were to who we are now. When our new identity in Christ comes alive in us, something happens to our insecurities: They vanish. Boldness rises up within us. We begin to declare 2 Corinthians 5:17 over ourselves—"If anyone is in Christ, the new creation has come: The old has gone, the new is here!"—and we believe it. When this occurs, the wall of insecurity shatters to the ground. It cannot stand against the beauty of our resurrected life in Christ.

The story of Peter and Jesus is powerful. Days after Jesus' resurrection, Peter had an opportunity for redemption as he walked with the Lord after breakfast by the fire.

When they had finished eating, Jesus said to Simon Peter, "Simon son of John, do you love me more than these?"

"Yes, Lord," he said, "you know that I love you."

Jesus said, "Feed my lambs."

Again Jesus said, "Simon son of John, do you love me?"

He answered, "Yes, Lord, you know that I love you."

Jesus said, "Take care of my sheep."

The third time he said to him, "Simon son of John, do you love me?"

Peter was hurt because Jesus asked him the third time, "Do you love me?" He said, "Lord, you know all things; you know that I love you."

Jesus said, "Feed my sheep. Very truly I tell you, when you were younger you dressed yourself and went where you wanted; but when you are old you will stretch out your hands, and someone else will dress you and lead you where you do not want to go." Jesus said this to indicate the kind of death by which Peter would glorify God. Then he said to him, "Follow me!"

John 21:15–19

Jesus was affirming who Peter was, and saying that he would indeed take up his cross in order to follow Him.

My friend, what beauty there is for you to learn who you are—a chosen, blood-bought daughter of the living God! What could be more beautiful?

Does it mean you will never again struggle with insecurity? Unfortunately, no, it does not mean you will no longer wrestle with this very real emotion. What it does mean is that you are empowered with the right tools to bring that wall to the ground, and then to continue moving forward. The lie that "there must be something wrong with me" loses its power and no longer prevents you from moving forward.

Insecurity can still creep in from time to time, but that is just the voice of the accuser trying to reassemble the wall in an effort to keep you stuck. Use what the Word of God says about you to silence that voice, and you will continue moving forward, full of the joy of Jesus, alive, bold and free.

The Trap

The trap is set when you believe the enemy's false narrative over your identity—that there is something wrong with you. To cause you to feel "less than" and to feel justified in believing there must be something wrong with you. This lays the foundation for that wall of insecurity. Before you know it, you are slamming into it each time you try to step forward, full of faith and ready to move mountains. The voice of the accuser swoops in and, because of the nature of insecurity, does not need to work too hard to convince you of his lies.

When you come into agreement with the lie of insecurity, you shrink back, convinced that there really is something wrong with you.

What is insecurity, anyway? The dictionary defines *insecurity* as "a state or feeling of anxiety, fear or self-doubt." Maya Angelou said, "The real difficulty is to overcome how you think about yourself."[2]

The Wall Shatters

The wall shatters when you believe who God says you are— unique and close to His heart. One of a kind. Fearfully and wonderfully made.

Peter's wall shattered as he walked with Jesus after breakfast by the fire and was recommissioned as a disciple. Jesus gave him a second chance, which is what Jesus' death was all about. When we get it wrong, Jesus is there to make it right. Sure, we

---

2. "Maya Angelou on Haters, Life, Reading, and Love," Farnam Street Media, September 2014, https://fs.blog/maya-angelou-on-haters-life-reading-and-love/.

will still face the natural consequences of our actions, but the internal washing away of our sins, making us clean and new, is powerful and beautiful.

The bottom line: You don't have to live insecure.

You don't.

You can live fully alive and free because of who Jesus says you are. He believes in you enough to pursue you with His love and wash you in His amazing grace.

The outcome of Peter's heart connection as a disciple of Christ? His voice was restored. He became a trumpet of truth and saw the first wave of conversions to Christianity reported in the book of Acts.

> Peter stood up with the Eleven, raised his voice and addressed the crowd: "Fellow Jews and all of you who live in Jerusalem, let me explain this to you; listen carefully to what I say."
>
> Acts 2:14

Peter declared boldly to the crowd on the Day of Pentecost who Jesus was: "God has made this Jesus, whom you crucified, both Lord and Messiah" (verse 36). He made no apologies about his affiliation with Jesus. To the multitude he declared, "Repent and be baptized" (verse 38). How could Peter be so bold? Because he had been set free from his insecurity. Awakening to who Jesus was and what Jesus said about him shattered that wall to the ground. The lie that "there must be something wrong with me" was dismantled into shards as he rose in boldness and in the power of God. He knew who he was.

Friend, this freedom is available to you as well. You can live free from the lie of "There must be something wrong with me" as you step into your beautiful identity as unique, one of a kind, no one else like you, a lover of Jesus.

Make that heart connection run deep today as you declare over yourself one more time, "Jesus loves me so much. I am a beautiful daughter of the King."

Moving Forward

Because I have wrestled with insecurity most of my life, I know what a sneaky enemy it is. It is built as a wall brick by brick as we believe the lie that says, "There's something wrong with you." Before we know it, we are slamming into this wall every time we try to move forward, convinced that there *is* something wrong with us. Why bother?

As I have drawn closer and closer to Jesus, I have experienced this wall shattering to the ground. It happens as His voice and what He says about me drowns out the lie of the enemy. You see, the wall of insecurity (like the other walls) is vulnerable. It is vulnerable to truth.

The Bible says, "If the Son sets you free, you will be free indeed" (John 8:36). When we press into the heart of God, hear His voice and encounter His transforming presence from the inside out, the shackles of insecurity are broken and the wall shatters to the ground.

Believe What God Says about You

You are God's chosen treasure—priests who are kings, a spiritual "nation" set apart as God's devoted ones. He called you out of darkness to experience his marvelous light, and now he claims you as his very own. He did this so that you would broadcast his glorious wonders throughout the world.

1 Peter 2:9 TPT

Jesus Says: You are of inestimable value. Your identity is found in Me. You are Mine.

Declare It: I am God's chosen treasure. I am of inestimable value. I am loved by Jesus.

Apply It: Speak truth over yourself today and each day forward. Write down the areas in which you feel insecure and then, using your red pen, write, "I am God's chosen treasure" next to each one. As you hear that pesky voice of the accuser telling you who you are, making you feel "less than," speak the truth of God's Word "I am not a slave to fear. I am a child of God."

Prayer

Father, wrap me in Your presence today and speak into my life Your words of truth. Who do You say that I am? I am listening.

3

Someone Else Can Do It Better

REALLY, LORD . . . ME? *Surely someone else can do it better.*

This was the conversation I had with the Lord as the dream to write a book surfaced after nearly ten years on the shelf. You know the shelf—that figurative place where we stick all the impossible, "maybe someday" dreams. We see the shelf accumulating item after item, dream after dream, and we wonder as the years slip away, *Will I ever do anything with those items on the shelf? Those dreams?*

When the day comes and the Lord asks you to pull one of those dreams off the shelf, what do you do? Do you go for it? Or are you like me and wrestle and resist just enough for the angst of the struggle to cause you to justify keeping the dream safely on the shelf "for now."

Why? Well, let's be raw and real here, friend. Often it is because we entertain the question, *Why me?* Why would God ask this of someone like me? You know—*me*, with all my flaws, limitations, questions, issues. . . . And then, *bam!*—enter that knockout statement: *Someone else can do it better.* We are convinced the dream is not for us. It cannot be.

This was me as I held my baby girl in my arms one night, crying out to God and calling my entire identity into question. My identity as the hardest worker in the room, the one climbing the corporate ladder, the workaholic, the "she'll get it done whatever it takes," go-to gal. The identity I had spent years building for myself was crumbling and I no longer knew how to see myself.

Here I was, a new mom, experiencing more love for another human being than I had ever known. But suddenly I no longer wanted the things I had been working so hard to get. It just wasn't me anymore.

Not the status.

Not the recognition.

Not even the financial reward that would come as a result of all my hard work.

Don't get me wrong—I am not saying don't go after any of those things. What I am saying is that my identity had become so rooted in them that no longer desiring them was scary. I had been working hard for years to get them. Who would I be without them?

But as I stared down at my firstborn in the dark of the night, I knew things were about to change and I was in for an uncharted, seemingly scary adventure with Jesus.

As I sought the Lord for what to do now, the answer was twofold. One, I would focus on being a mom. And two, there was that dream He was showing me—that dusty old dream of writing a book that I had placed on the shelf for an entire decade. God was showing me this in the dark of the night as all my ambitions were crumbling to the ground.

After the Lord called this new mom to pursue her book dream, I spent nearly two more years wrestling with the mindset that "someone else can do it better." Living in Fargo, North Dakota, we were barely plugged into our church at the time. I had no connections. I had never met another person who had written a book. Authors seemed fancy and put together, while I was trying to remember to fold my laundry and plan dinner.

Yet when I closed my eyes, I could see myself as God saw me. I could hear His voice calling me *Author*. I could see the faces of the people my books would reach. I could remember the call from the decade prior when He had said, *Krissy, I want you to write a book for your generation*. So I went for it.

I mentioned earlier that, through the process of writing, I overcame mindsets I did not realize I still had. One of those mindsets (which we discussed in chapter 1) was "I'm just not enough"—a form of shame for my inadequacies. But another one was the "someone else can do it better" mindset and the wall of comparison. Now, as I wrote, that wall shattered to the ground.

It has been more than ten years since this moment, and I can tell you that what you hold in your hands is the fruit of the wall of comparison shattering to the ground. This is my third book in ten years, and I have much more to give. I even have the privilege of teaching others how to write books and overcome their own debilitating mindsets. I have seen hundreds of aspiring authors get started on their "book babies," as I call them, and dozens of new authors publishing their first book in just my first two years of teaching what I have learned.

In the spirit of full disclosure, however, I want you to know that the lie of "someone else can do it better" continues to run through my mind as I tackle new projects, especially "God projects"—things that are way bigger than me, so I know they are God, because I would never have signed up for it on my own (wink, wink!). The enemy tries to halt us at every turn, and does not like to see us making progress, because we begin believing what God says about us. He will use anything he can to build up this wall of comparison, so we never feel we are quite enough, or the right one to answer God's call on our life. We become like Moses, objecting to the assignment because of our personal limits or weaknesses. (We are going to look at him a little later in this chapter.)

Additional lies to look out for:

- You're not qualified.
- You're not educated enough.
- You're too old.
- You're too young.
- You've missed it; it's too late.

What are some others? Write down in your journal the lies you have dealt with or are dealing with.

The Wall: Comparison

The dictionary defines *comparison* as "examining two or more items to establish similarities and dissimilarities." We tend to look for superiority or inferiority. Comparison is the thing that keeps us on the other side of our destiny.

How do you like that for a bold statement? But I had to go for it with this one. Why? Because comparison is the enemy's tool to rob not only you but God.

I am full of bold statements today, my friend, because I am not messing around with this wall of comparison anymore. I have tiptoed around it for too many years, and frankly, I am over it. Comparison has done nothing but steal from my life. It has kept me from moving forward completely into God's plans as I fiddle around with those pesky lies the enemy uses as building blocks for the wall of comparison. Lies like *Someone else can do it better*. Sound familiar?

Our inner dialogue sounds a lot like this:

- Someone else can do it better.
- She is way more qualified than I am.
- She has way more influence than I do.
- She's a better communicator than I am.
- I could never do what she does
- She doesn't struggle the way I do.
- I see others making the progress I wish I could make.

The Trap

The trap is set when we become stuck on the hamster wheel of comparison so we never really move forward in life. Why does the enemy want us to buy into the lie of *Someone else can do it better*? Because when we do, we forfeit our destiny.

Yep, sorry (but not sorry) to say it. It is true and needs to be said so you can be free. Think about the aim of this lie. When you believe it, you end up taking a backseat to what God has called you to do while allowing someone else to do it instead.

Ouch. I know. But hang in there —there is hope.

Maybe you are called to start a business, or write a book, or start a Bible study in your neighborhood, or set up a meal train for a friend or neighbor who has just had surgery—or maybe it is simply to speak up more and be a voice of truth to the lost around you. Whatever it is—if you continue in the mindset of *Someone else can do it better*, then you will be stuck behind this wall of comparison long term, never actually feeling as if you are the right one to do what God is calling you to do.

There are two drivers for comparison in your life: the world around you, and you yourself.

The world will compare you to others. It is second nature. We all do it, at least on a subconscious level.

Then there is your own self-examination, as you compare yourself to others. Call it flesh, call it the voice of the enemy. Whatever you call it, we all seem to do it, some of us more than others. If you have come this far in this chapter, I suspect you are finding common ground.

The bottom line is this: Comparison is a wall built by the lie we buy into that others can do it better.

The Wall Shatters

The wall shatters when we declare from the depths of our hearts, "I can do all things through Christ who strengthens me" (Philippians 4:13 NKJV)—and mean it. There is no one better to fulfill the call of God on your life than you, my friend.

Listen—before we continue, there is something you need to know about me. I have a fire in my bones to see the women of God rising to their highest potential in the Kingdom of God. To see an army of humble, "laid-down lovers of Jesus" (as Heidi Baker says), no longer afraid, no longer holding back, running full speed ahead in the amazing God call on their life. I have seen too many women, friends, sisters holding back over the years, and it breaks my heart. It is time for God's daughters to see themselves the way God sees them, breaking down those walls while running wild and free in the Kingdom.

This describes you, my friend . . . my sister. Yes—*you*. You did not pick up this book by chance. You were selected as one of the many readers who is a sister in the army God is igniting. It is time for you to say goodbye to what holds you back, shatter those walls and fulfill His assignment on your life. It is time to believe what God says about you.

He calls you daughter.

Beloved.

Friend.

He says you are a champion.

Unique.

One of a kind.

He is saying over you now, *Stop comparing yourself to your sister on your right or on your left, and stop comparing yourself to the women leaders whose books you read or whose sermons you watch. The main difference between them and you is that they decided to stop listening to the lies and move forward. Now is your chance to do the same. So arise and shine, My beloved. I am with you and am calling you forward—out of the cave and into My marvelous light.*

The wall of comparison shatters as you believe what God says about you. Once and for all.

Take a moment and allow His presence to flood over you now. Listen as the Lord speaks a word of hope over you. Be sure and write down what you hear Him say.

Moving Forward

Moses was quite the deflector—unsure for a long time about who God had made him to be, and then trying to get out of his calling to lead God's people out of Egypt. But God pursued him. We read about Moses' experience in the desert when God appeared to him in the burning bush. God was commissioning him to be His mouthpiece to Pharaoh to free His people from slavery and bring them into the Promised Land.

I'm Not Enough

Can you imagine? You are out for a walk one night and you see one of the bushes in the neighbor's yard on fire. You move toward it to see what is going on, when you hear the voice of God calling your name. *Take off your shoes, [insert your name]. You are standing on holy ground.*

Wowzah! What would you do?

I think I would be terrified at first, but I would approach the bush and remove my shoes as instructed. I would likely fall to my knees while I was at it. What an experience! Sometimes I wonder if this is what it would take for me to finally start agreeing with who God says I am a little more quickly. Perhaps if I had an encounter like this, I would not be so fast to doubt Him when He says to me, *Krissy, you can do what I'm calling you to do—you can!—because it's Christ in you.* Right?

The point is, God made Himself very real to Moses, leaving no room for Moses to question if it was Him or not. Yet somehow Moses still managed to question God's instruction, and he actually resisted letting who God said he was sink in deep, and then cooperating with the call.

God said to Moses:

> "The cry of the Israelites has reached me, and I have seen the way the Egyptians are oppressing them. So now, go. I am sending you to Pharaoh to bring my people the Israelites out of Egypt."
>
> But Moses said to God, "Who am I that I should go to Pharaoh and bring the Israelites out of Egypt?"
>
> Exodus 3:9–11

Maybe Moses missed the latest Bible teaching that says, "God doesn't call the qualified; He qualifies the called."

I am being humorous here, but also serious. The fun thing is that it is from Moses' story (and the stories of other leaders in

52

the Bible) that we glean this insight. Moses' objections to his call teach us that God does not need us to be perfect to use us; He will perfect us as we go. But we must be willing to go—to partner with what God is saying about us, stop resisting and then obey His call.

Even after God promised Moses, "I will be with you" (verse 12), and told Moses His name, and gave him miraculous signs to show the Egyptians, Moses continued to resist.

> "Pardon your servant, Lord. I have never been eloquent, neither in the past nor since you have spoken to your servant. I am slow of speech and tongue."
>
> The LORD said to him, "Who gave human beings their mouths? Who makes them deaf or mute? Who gives them sight or makes them blind? Is it not I, the LORD? Now go; I will help you speak and will teach you what to say."
>
> But Moses said, "Pardon your servant, Lord. Please send someone else."
>
> Exodus 4:10–13

Moses was comparing himself to the kind of person who, in his view, would be more qualified to deliver the word of the Lord and lead His people out of Egypt. Someone eloquent of speech, someone who spoke faster than he did. He was comparing himself to an ideal, when God was looking at Moses and saying, *You are the ideal.*

Why was Moses God's ideal choice to speak to Pharaoh? Because of his weakness. The very limitation Moses argued counted him out—his lack of eloquence—was the very reason God knew He could use him. Because Moses had a limitation, he would need to rely on God fully to deliver His words and lead His people. (And actually God gave him a helper, his brother, Aaron, to help him speak.)

Paul said it best: "I will boast all the more gladly about my weaknesses, so that Christ's power may rest on me" (2 Corinthians 12:9).

My dad, Dr. James Torkildson, a psychologist and amazing man of God, says, "Our limits become guideposts for our need for God."

Do you see the pattern here, my friend? Stop comparing yourself to the "ideal" person you think would be more qualified to move forward with what God has called you to. Instead, believe what God says about you and partner with Him. He calls you perfect just as you are because He sees you through the perfection of Christ, and because, in your limits, you will rely all the more on Jesus' strength operating through you.

I need Jesus desperately for everything He has called me to. I would never have dreamed I would be doing the things I am doing now. With some of what I have my hands in now, I go, "Only You, Jesus." But He has made it clear to me that this is His call, so I say, "Okay, Lord. I will cooperate with You. But I am very needy because I know I can't do any of this without Your constant help and support."

And you know what I have learned in the process? He loves it! He loves every second of my neediness, my total dependence on Him. He is smiling and saying, *She's finally getting it. It's not about her perfection. It's about My grace and My perfection.*

Back to that mindset, *Someone else can do it better*—allow me to let you in on a little secret. God thought the same thing, and then pointed at you. God says, "You can." He knows you can because you will let go and allow Him to operate through you as you partner with what He says about you.

Can you hear this wall of comparison shattering to the ground? I can! Close your eyes now and listen. I know you will hear it, too.

Believe What God Says about You

I can do all things through Christ who strengthens me.

Philippians 4:13 NKJV

Jesus Says: I am strong where you are weak.

Declare It: In my weakness, His power is made perfect. I can do all things through Christ who gives me strength.

Apply It: Write down the areas where you have compared yourself to others. In just a few words, describe those areas. And when you are finished with your list, take a red pen and write the words, "I can—through Christ."

Prayer

Father, shatter the wall of comparison to the ground as I believe what You are saying over me today. Empower me to embrace my weakness as Paul did so I can allow Your power and strength to surge through me. Wash over me with Your truth. I believe that I am called, beloved and qualified, ready and able to move forward in my life just as I am. In Jesus' mighty name. Amen.

PART 2

I'm Afraid

Definition of *fear*

1. An unpleasant emotion caused by being aware of danger.
2. A feeling of being afraid.

Mindsets

1. I'm so afraid.
2. But I might fail.
3. I don't want to ruffle any feathers.

Walls

1. Fear
2. Fear of failure
3. People pleasing

4

I'm So Afraid

I HAVE WALKED in fear most of my life.

There. I said it. It has taken me a long time to be able to just say it, but now, finally, I am on the other side of fear. I can look back and say, "Oh, yeah, *that* was fear, and *that* was fear . . ." and so on.

I have experienced such breakthrough from the grip of fear that I even wrote a book about it, *Slaying the Giant of Fear.* In it I explore how and why the enemy uses fear as one of his greatest weapons against the people of God, and I explore the divine weaponry we have been given to slay this giant once and for all.

My journey with fear began with the fear of man, also known as people pleasing (which I unpack further in chapter 6). Over time that tendency grew into such fear that I became paralyzed, stalled out, stuck. In fact, I was so gripped by fear that my entire body began to shut down. My adrenal system was shot; my nervous system was on overload, sending shock waves throughout my body at random moments; and, according to my physician, my cortisol levels had plummeted. I was living in total fear.

It was not as though I was facing anything life-threatening. I was dealing with emotional issues, including a constant state of anxiety, which in turn became fear. Eventually "I'm so afraid" became my constant statement and day-to-day MO (mode of operating). Afraid of what? Of everything, it would seem. I had become paralyzed by the fear of saying the wrong thing, doing the wrong thing and letting people down. Whereas once I had experienced a childlike zeal for ministry, the enemy replaced that with anxiety and fear that, at any point, I might disqualify myself from the race.

I was not concerned that I might have some major moral failure. No, what I feared was that I would say or do something the wrong way. I saw firsthand the power that a naysayer or nitpicker could have in my life. What some might consider just a little bit of "constructive" feedback—which I should be able to receive or simply move beyond—had blown up into a collection of unsolicited opinions by way of social media. Simple little statements had now become the voice of the giant of fear roaring over my life: *Who do you think you are? What are you doing here? You are being ridiculous! No one really cares.* It took years for me to step forward across the battle line into God's destiny of peace and freedom.

When you begin taking steps forward into God's call on your life, people like to weigh in. Some thoughts are good, some not so good. The more I wrote and spoke and stood for truth, the more people came out of the woodwork to voice their views. Most were acquaintances, people I barely knew, friends of friends of friends. As an only child and introvert, I live a pretty simple life. Donovan and I are homebodies and each other's best friend, and I was new to the social media scene and not used to all the noise out there. Yikes! Everyone seemed to be examining motives: *What is your motive for writing a book? What is your motive for holding a conference? Are you pursuing selfish ambition? Are you prideful or self-seeking?*

All I knew was that I had been stuck for nearly two decades, unsure about myself and convinced I had missed God's call on my life. After spending years in the workforce and then having children, I was once again captivated by God, for the first time since I was a fifteen-year-old girl encountering the bigness and love of my heavenly Father. Running forward into His call and plan for my life, I felt as though I had slipped into who He made me to be.

I never set out to start a ministry. I simply sat down at the kitchen table during my children's naptime and started writing. *Do something* was the constant declarative statement from the Holy Spirit for months leading up to that simple yet monumental moment. Have you ever experienced this? A word or phrase seems to keep coming up and you know God is trying to get your attention? Well, my attention He had, and on January 7, 2012, I sat down at the kitchen table and started writing while my newborn and my toddler shared a naptime—which in those days was a miracle in itself.

Just sit down and start writing was another phrase that kept coming to mind. And a third one: *If not now, when?*

So you can see why, on this miraculous day when both of my kiddos were asleep on a cold, snowy day, tucked away in my little house in my little town of Fargo, North Dakota, I recognized the divine appointment and complied. Simply and purely, I did something. Now was the time. I sat down and started writing.

And a couple of years later, once we had uprooted our family and relocated to the Panhandle of Florida to live closer to my mom and grandparents, a ministry was born.

As I said, I never set out to start a ministry. When I am asked today, "How do I start a ministry?" my answer remains, "I really don't know. Do . . . *something?*"

We need only follow the breadcrumbs dropped before us by our heavenly Father as He leads us forward into His amazing plans for our life. "'I know the plans I have for you,' declares the LORD, 'plans to prosper you and not to harm you, plans to give you hope and a future'" (Jeremiah 29:11).

Over the next several years, the Lord led me beautifully and purely by the hand, one simple step at a time, into His call on my life.

It still surprises me how quickly the fear set in. It happened after I blogged about a retail store in the mall that had placed signage in their storefront window with images of the middle finger being raised. Working at a jewelry store at the time, I was mortified to observe families and children walking past this store seeing the middle finger on full display, and I felt a fire within me to *do something*. So I wrote an article about it on my blog, which God used miraculously to get the attention of the vice president of operations for the retail chain. Within 24 hours she emailed me, requesting a meeting. The outcome: Within 72 hours of posting the article on my little blog, all two hundred–plus stores nationwide removed this signage from their window.

Mover, shaker, history-maker were words spoken over my life at fifteen, just prior to my life-changing encounter with God. Now I began seeing signs of these words. But, as it goes with the enemy, he was quick to enlist negative, opposing voices that sparked a spiral effect of anxiety and panic and ultimately jumpstarted my battle with fear, which would last the next several years of my life.

You know who the opposing voices were? Fellow believers. This was my first encounter with fellow believers who, for whatever reason, decided to wage an all-out attack on me for my efforts to see victory over this vulgar display in the store window. The comments came flooding in. "You're being ridiculous," some said. "Don't you have better things to do with your time?"

Private messages, emails, responses to my Facebook posts, comments on my blog—I was inundated by believers, many of whom I knew. I could understand nonbelievers being irritated at my efforts, but it was those I thought were my brothers and sisters in Christ who ended up causing the most damage to my heart.

I thought I was doing a good thing, operating in simple obedience to the voice of my Father. The retail store was located in front of my store, which I would probably not have seen otherwise. For me, then, it was strategic of the Lord, not to mention fruitful, because the issue was resolved on a national scale in just three days. But the bullying and cruelty of others lasted long after those three days.

"This has already been resolved. We were victorious. It's over. Move on." This is what I wanted to say to the hundreds of naysayers. Instead I ignored them, and eventually removed the blog post from my website and deleted mention of it on my Facebook profile and page. This also led to my going off social media completely for two years. I was tired of all the noise and just needed to heal. It felt as if that innocent place where I had started had been compromised. My joy was gone, and in its place, debilitating anxiety and the fear of saying the wrong thing, offending people and getting it wrong.

The Wall: Fear

Fear is a sneaky enemy. Often (as I said) we don't even know it is fear until it has gripped us to our core. By that time we feel trapped behind the bars of worry, anxiety and, yes, fear. The enemy revels in using fear to stop God's people from moving forward. He has used it since the beginning of time when he deceived Adam and Eve through the fear of missing out. He convinced them to believe they were missing out on something good by not eating of the other tree, the one God commanded them not to eat of.

There are many types of fear: fear of failure, fear of missing out, fear of death, fear of public speaking. . . . The list goes on and on. In this chapter I will discuss fear in general and allow you to fill in the blank of the specific aspect of fear you deal with in your personal journey.

The dictionary defines *fear* as "an unpleasant emotion caused by being aware of danger." Fear robs us. It halts us in our journey into all that God has planned for us. It inhibits us from hearing Him clearly as He speaks life, truth and hope over us and who we are. It plugs our ears to truth so all we hear are the lies. Lies like:

- You're unqualified.
- Who do you think you are?
- You're incapable.
- You might lose everything if you try.
- You should just quit.

I have heard just about every lie there is when it comes to my identity as God's daughter.

- You're not pretty enough.
- You're not educated enough.
- You don't have enough resources.
- You missed the mark.

- You should have started sooner.
- It's too late.
- You're too young.
- You're too old.

Need I continue? You get the point. I am sure by now you have inserted a few of the lies you have entertained over the years as well. Isn't it amazing how much chatter we listen to as time goes by? I mean, really, when we stop, as we are doing right now, and take inventory of the lies we have believed, it seems almost ridiculous that we would buy into such statements that contradict what God says about us. When we are in reflection mode, it is easy to see. So why do we find ourselves buying into obvious deceptions?

I think it is all about the timing. The enemy is strategic and sets in motion these triggers so he can strike at the most opportune moment—when we are most vulnerable.

The Trap

The trap is set for times when we are exhausted, emotional or stressed. The Bible compares the devil to a lion.

Think about lions for a moment. When they hunt, they are very patient. They seek out their prey and even customize their attack based on the size of the animal, its strength and the size of its community. The lioness will hunt alone and hide in the grass, waiting patiently for the prey to come close enough; then she will strike. If hunting an animal in a herd, she will pursue it with other lions, circle the prey and bring chaos to the herd in order to break it up, isolating the small and weak.[3]

3. "How Do Lions Hunt? Know Their Hunting Tactics," Snow Africa Adventures, 2020, https://snowafricaadventure.com/blog/hunting-strategy-of-the-lions.

The apostle Peter compares the devil to a lion in his strategic approach to seek out his prey and strike when his target is most vulnerable, anxious or isolated. You can see how efficient the enemy is. He is cold and calculating. This is why Peter implores us to be alert and ready. But he sandwiches this warning between two powerful tools for us to use:

> Cast all your anxiety on [God] because he cares for you. Be alert and of sober mind. Your enemy the devil prowls around like a roaring lion looking for someone to devour. Resist him, standing firm in the faith.
>
> 1 Peter 5:7–9

We are to cast all our cares, worries and fears onto God because He cares for us. We are to be alert and clear-headed, ready to resist the enemy when he strikes by standing firm in our faith—steadfast, unwavering, secure in Christ, knowing it is the Lord who fights our battles (see Deuteronomy 3:22).

You can see how the enemy calculates his moves. Like the lion, he is patient. He awaits those moments when life happens and your guard is down. Maybe you get a call from a family member who is not in good health, or you are turned down for a promotion at work and you are in shock. Or perhaps you are taking faith steps forward in your calling and you are surprised by the unsolicited opinions and oppositions of others. The invitation from the Father is to cast those cares on Him; but often we delay or carry the burden longer than we should. We become discouraged, frustrated, worried about the future. The enemy waits for us to become so weary with sadness or riddled with anxiety that he strikes and begins to whisper a lie—*See, bad things always happen to you!*—and we are pierced with fear. We experience that chill down our spines and declare, "I'm so afraid."

Fear is a trap the enemy sets for us so that we will perpetually face this wall and agree with the lie that life will always be this way, I will always be afraid, and moving forward is impossible. We feel as if we have taken one step forward only to go two back. Can you relate to this?

Let's not forget Peter's instruction: "Resist [the devil], standing firm in the faith" (1 Peter 5:9). Stand firm today; God is with you. He will never leave you or forsake you. You do not have to battle fear for the rest of your life. Resist—again and again. Resist.

The Wall Shatters

The wall shatters when we arise in our full identity as daughters of God—when we stand firm in who God says we are, as over against who the enemy attempts to make us into: weak, puny, insignificant and helpless. The story of David and Goliath in the Bible is the perfect illustration.

In 1 Samuel 17 we see the army of Israel lined up for battle against the Philistine army. God had already anointed David to be king, but he was still a teenager, tending sheep in his father's field. His father asked him to bring food to his older brothers on the battlefield, soldiers in King Saul's army, and report back with news of how they were doing. Typical father stuff, right?

As David arrived on the field, he caught wind of a crisis. A Philistine warrior, a fearsome giant, had drawn up his battle line and challenged any of the Israelite soldiers to take him on. The giant was more than nine feet tall, wore bronze armor and carried a staff in his hand that was nearly twelve feet long. His shouts echoed throughout the valley and pierced the hearts of the soldiers with fear.

Goliath stood and shouted to the ranks of Israel, "Why do you come out and line up for battle? Am I not a Philistine, and are

I'm Afraid

you not the servants of Saul? . . . This day I defy the armies of
Israel! Give me a man and let us fight each other."

1 Samuel 17:8, 10

"Why have you come?" What a question to ask an army!
This was the start of the demoralization of the entire force—
including their leader, King Saul. Can you imagine? You show
up for the event you have been training for and are asked,
"What are you doing here?" I don't know about you but
that would be enough right there to make me question my
abilities.

But Goliath was not asking; he was imparting. He was de-
positing lies into the hearts of the soldiers in God's army, de-
moralizing them from within, messing with their minds, so they
would lose confidence and give up. He presented himself as an
impenetrable force; he could not be beaten. And this occurred
morning and evening for forty days and forty nights. Over and
over, on repeat.

How often do we experience that with fear? We may wake
up and decide, *I'm not going to allow fear to shut me down
any longer. Today I'm moving forward.* And then, *boom!* That
same old mindset resounds in our hearts: *I'm so afraid. I'll try
again tomorrow. Today is just not the day.*

The mindset of "I can't!" builds and reinforces the wall of
fear. And if we don't grab hold of what God is exhorting us—"I
can do all things through Christ who strengthens me" (Philippians 4:13 NKJV)—we will be stuck behind the wall of fear all
our days.

This is what was occurring with the army of God. They
had forgotten who they were and who fought their battles for
them—the Lord Almighty, *Jehovah Sabaoth,* Hebrew for "the
Lord of Hosts" or "the Lord of Armies." Saul and all the Israelites were "dismayed and terrified" (1 Samuel 17:11).

One of the meanings of the word *dismay* in Hebrew is "to be shattered."[4] Saul and his entire army were shattered from within as this Philistine giant defied their identities as soldiers and champions of the living God. Goliath was challenging their value as warriors, and ultimately defying God almighty—which was exactly David's perspective when he came on the scene. Indignant, he asked them, "Who is this uncircumcised Philistine that he should defy the armies of the living God?" (verse 26).

We know from the Scriptures that David walked in fellowship with God. He knew God's powerful hand of protection personally, which he recounted to King Saul as he pleaded with him to let him fight the giant and take him down, in order to restore glory to God.

David did not need earthly assurances, comforts or even tools. He declined Saul's armor and showed up to the battle line carrying only what he already had. Yes, he reached into the stream and pulled out five smooth stones, but those stones were for the slingshot he already had in his possession.

David presented himself before this giant of fear as a man after God's own heart (see 1 Samuel 13:14). He knew without a doubt that God would protect him; he needed only to declare what God was saying—to declare the truth boldly to the one spewing lies over God's people.

> David said to the Philistine, "You come against me with sword and spear and javelin, but I come against you in the name of the Lord Almighty, the God of the armies of Israel, whom you have defied. This day the Lord will deliver you into my hands."
>
> 1 Samuel 17:45–46

The wall of fear shatters as we partner with truth in the face of lies—as we stand firm on who God is and what God says about us.

4. Bible Hub, s.v. "2865.chathath," https://biblehub.com/hebrew/2865.htm.

Do you know what the Lord showed me about this story? David was without fear. He was not even there to fight; he had come there to serve, bringing food to his brothers. And he showed up at the battle line unassuming and unafraid. The Israelite army, by contrast, is an example of our natural, human response to fear. They were intimidated and shut down by the giant's rants, crushed from within. Our natural, human response is to believe the lies and run away. But David is an example of a Holy Spirit–inspired response.

Friend, what is He saying to you now? Take a moment and face that giant of fear. Decide today that you will dive more deeply into God's heart for you, so that the mindset of *I'm so afraid* is replaced by *Jesus fights my battles for me. I am not afraid*. Listen as that wall of fear begins to shatter even now. Can you hear it cracking?

Here's a key: David knew who he was in the Lord because of his deep relationship with Him, and the result was a headless giant of fear and the entire army awakening to their identity as the army of the Lord.

So David triumphed over the Philistine with a sling and a stone; without a sword in his hand he struck down the Philistine and killed him.

David ran and stood over him. He took hold of the Philistine's sword and drew it from the sheath. After he killed him, he cut off his head with the sword.

When the Philistines saw that their hero was dead, they turned and ran. Then the men of Israel and Judah surged forward with a shout.

1 Samuel 17:50–52

The wall of fear shattered to the ground as they surged forward with a shout!

Believe What God Says about You

God has not given us a spirit of fear, but of power and of love and of a sound mind.

2 Timothy 1:7 NKJV

Jesus Says: You don't need to fear. I am with you always.

Declare It: I am not afraid. I am bold and courageous.

Apply It: Stand up in your room right now, wherever you are. Close your eyes and picture what you fear the most—that which you feel (or know) holds you back. Now speak right to it: "I am not afraid. I am bold and courageous!"

Prayer

Father, I desire an increase of boldness, courage and faith today as I take steps forward in the right direction. Steps of faith. Steps of courage. Steps of life! Breathe on me now a fresh wind of hope—I am not afraid anymore, in Jesus' mighty name.

5

But I Might Fail

I HAVE PURSUED A VARIETY of endeavors over the last twenty years, and every time I leap into something new, a pesky, often paralyzing question arises: *But what if I fail?* This question lingers as long as I allow it to.

While there is some validity in asking the question, being motivated by the fear of failure is contrary to the Word of God.

Over the years I feel I have established a healthy outlook on what I consider "success." I don't worry so much anymore about what the results look like. To me, success is found in my obedience to the call. If I do my best, keep trying, remain teachable and keep moving forward, positive results often follow. Even if the results aren't what I may have hoped for, with the Lord there's always a learning opportunity to be found.

But this wasn't always the case. Before I left the workforce to become a stay-at-home mom, I worked long hours and was gripped by the fear of failure. I struggled to strike the right balance between my own view of success and failure with the importance of producing results and improving my company's return on investment.

As a young business professional in the fitness industry, I worked hard to grow our business, bring on new customers, train the team and deliver results to our corporate headquarters. I found it challenging to feel good about my efforts and often wondered, *Is my best enough?*

As a young leader with a lot of responsibility on my shoulders, I struggled hugely on how to reconcile doing my best with my best maybe not being enough—and I was filled with fear. Alarm bells began sounding in my heart and mind, and my body was filled with distress.

My inner dialogue sounded a lot like this:

- What if my best isn't good enough?
- What if people don't like it?
- What if it isn't profitable?
- So much is riding on this!
- What will happen to our business?
- What will happen to our team?
- What impact could this have on my family?

My heart is still racing as I reflect on this very stressful time in my life. *Deep breath, Krissy. Inhale . . . exhale.*

Let me tell you, flourishing from this frame of mind is nearly impossible. There is way too much pressure, way too much stress.

But how do we avoid this thinking when the reality is, we really *do* need to deliver something? Our word was given, a contract was signed, whatever the case may be. A deliverable is expected. It might be a project at work, a report that is due, a meeting you are preparing for, a project at home, something you are working on for your kids or family. It can be anything, really. The enemy uses the mindset *I might fail* to aid in constructing the wall of fear in our lives.

My dad, Dr. James Torkildson (the psychologist and amazing man of God I quoted in chapter 3), has said to me my entire life, "Krissy, your job isn't to worry about the outcome. Your job is to simply do what's right. Leave the outcome to the Lord." We say goodbye to the fear of failure as we release the results of our efforts to Father God.

Let's look a little closer at this wall.

The Wall: Fear of Failure

Psychology Today defines *fear of failure* as "the underlying feeling that 'if I make a mistake, I will disappoint people and/or be punished.'"[5] Our inner dialogue sounds a lot like this:

- I can't do this.
- Just look at how many times I've failed already.
- Everybody else can do it. I'm the problem.
- It's not even worth trying again.
- What if I get it wrong?
- What if I make a mistake?

The fear of failure is a common motivator to many; in fact, our society even seems to perpetuate this fear. Many of us live with debt hanging over our heads—mortgages, car leases, school tuitions and more. So much rides on the success of our endeavors that the fear of failure almost becomes second

5. Sherry Pagoto, Ph.D., "Are You a People Pleaser? How the Inability to Say 'No' Can Lead to Health Consequences," October 26, 2012, https://www.psychologytoday.com/us/blog/shrink/201210/are-you-people-pleaser.

nature. It is no wonder 78 percent of Americans say they are stressed out on a regular basis, and of this group, women make up the majority. At the time of this survey, April 2021, Gen Xers (those born between 1965 and 1980) were the most stressed generation.[6]

Honestly, just reading this study makes my heart race. There is something about the embrace of living stressed out and full of fear in our culture that tugs on my human tendency to be anxious.

Let's take a deep breath together and say, "Thank You, Jesus. You have created a better way for me."

Breathe, my friend . . . because as daughters of God, we do not need to live with this kind of anxiety, worry and fear.

Let's talk about what failure really is. *Failure* is defined as "falling short; being or becoming absent or inadequate; being unsuccessful." Much of the fear of failure is about simply falling short. And we don't have to miss the mark totally to feel we have failed. If we are off a little, we might write it off as a total loss.

Why do we do this? Because our thinking is rooted in fear and perfectionism. Ultimately we may be afraid to fail because we wonder, *What does that say about me?* We worry that it reflects on us as not good enough, not smart enough, not capable enough or whatever. If and when we experience what we consider a failure, it simply proves that our fear was valid.

I discussed this with my dad, Dr. James Torkildson. Here is what he said:

We need a better understanding of failure. It needs to be reframed and reconsidered in a more balanced term. The reality is,

6. Michelle Black, "Nearly 8 in 10 Americans Feel Stressed Weekly—and 1 in 7 Do Every Day," ValuePenguin/Lending Tree, April 5, 2021, https://www.value penguin.com/nearly-eight-in-ten-americans-feel-stress-weekly.

you *will* fail. People fail because they're human beings. There's nothing wrong with failure. It is our fear that cripples us. Failure itself is a reality, and it's going to happen to everyone many times in life.

You see, my friend, the problem is not really failure; it is our conception (misconception) of failure. Failure is a reality, as my dad says, something everyone experiences. There is nothing to fear, then, about failure. The only thing to fear is if we don't learn the lessons failure can teach us.

When my kids were little, I would always try to protect them from falling down or breaking a limb. Dad would say to me, "Krissy, people learn more through failure than through success." Think about that for a moment. If we tiptoe around failure too much, we miss many opportunities to learn and grow.

The bottom line: failure is not the problem; our overweighted association with failure as a negative is what makes us fearful.

The Trap

The trap is set when we put the wrong valuation on failure—when we see it as a negative proving that something is wrong with us. We focus so much on "me" that we miss the bigger picture—that God wants to use us just as we are, and that He uses failure as part of the journey in teaching us. We emphasize the outcome of our endeavors over our lifestyle of following after Jesus in obedience, putting all our trust in Him. The enemy is deceiving us with a crippling interpretation of failure—that it is somehow the be-all and end-all—when, in reality, failure is part of the journey.

The nature of the fear of failure is that we regard our own efforts and abilities over the supernatural ability of God. He can do anything. He can, and will, lift the burden from you as you cast your cares onto Him. But if we focus too much on the circumstances around us, and lose sight of the big picture, we are riddled with stress, pressure and fear. Our own achievements become our god, and our inner dialogue of worry drowns out the voice of our Lord.

Wow! What a trap this is, my friend. But we do not have to live like this. It is time to say goodbye to the wall of fear of failure.

The Wall Shatters

The wall shatters when we realize that Jesus is not looking for us to avoid failure; He is looking for us to move forward in obedience. He wants us to embrace failure as a normal part of the journey. "Failure," as my dad says, "is the process of improvement. It's an opportunity to move forward."

It is quite simple, really. Fix your eyes and ears on Jesus. What is He saying to you? Where is He leading you? What has He placed in you that you are compelled to pursue? Our focus determines our fears. Do we focus on what we fear the most? Or do we focus on the One motioning us forward despite fear?

Let's return to the apostle Peter at the moment when Jesus called him out of the boat to walk atop the waters with Him.

Talk about a "what-if-I-fail" moment! The repercussions of failure would be death. Peter would have been swallowed up by the waves had his feet not stayed on top of the waters supernaturally with Jesus.

> The boat was already a considerable distance from land, buffeted by the waves because the wind was against it. Shortly before dawn Jesus went out to them, walking on the lake. When the disciples saw him walking on the lake, they were terrified. "It's a ghost," they said, and cried out in fear.

But Jesus immediately said to them: "Take courage! It is I. Don't be afraid."

"Lord, if it's you," Peter replied, "tell me to come to you on the water."

"Come," he said.

Matthew 14:24–29

What was Peter thinking when he asked Jesus to call him out there with Him? What was inside him that would request such a thing?

I have to think it was trust. Trust that he knew Jesus enough to be sure Jesus would not call him out if He did not have a safe (albeit unconventional) pathway for him. Peter was modeling this trust without fear of outcome. He was not focusing on his own efforts. He knew that this simple act of obedience would trigger the supernatural empowering of the impossible. His simple act of obedience would tug at the heart of God, ensuring Peter's success.

And sure enough, "Peter got down out of the boat, walked on the water and came toward Jesus" (verse 29).

Can you imagine? Peter stepped out onto the choppy waters and began walking toward Jesus. One step in front of the other, staying on top of the water that had been buffeting the boat and causing all inside to fear, even though they were relatively safe inside the structure of their sturdy vessel. Now Peter was alone, walking on water, his eyes fixed on Jesus.

But as his focus shifted from Christ to the wind raging around him, and the rough water beneath his feet, he began to sink. I imagine his heart began to sink as well. His mind moved from *Jesus can do anything* to *What if I don't make it? What if I go down?* He went from "Jesus can" to "I can't," and his fear of failure brought doubt.

When he saw the wind, he was afraid and, beginning to sink, cried out, "Lord, save me!" Immediately Jesus reached out his hand and caught him. "You of little faith," he said, "why did you doubt?"

verses 30–31

Peter had made it all the way to Jesus. He had walked from the boat to His Lord, and as he stood before Jesus on the water, he allowed his focus to shift from the Lord to the outcome of his own actions: *I've come all this way. Now what? How can I possibly continue to stand? The wind is so strong. The storm is all around me. This is impossible! I'm going to sink.* And sink he did.

Can you relate to this feeling, my friend—the feeling that you have come so far, worked so hard, and now what? It is as if the grace that brought you to this point lifts just long enough for you to take a look around and realize, *Wow, I shouldn't be here*, and you shift your focus from Jesus to your circumstances. When the weight of the outcome shifts from Jesus to you, you are feeding this worry. Then that sinking feeling, the fear of failure, grips your heart, and you are not sure how to move forward.

This is the moment you ask Jesus for help. This is the time you say, like Peter, "Jesus, help!" And you experience Him reaching out His hand, just as He did for Peter, pulling you up from the sinking pit of fear and into the safety and security of His presence.

The bottom line is this: Our fear of failure is rooted in our worry over the outcome of our efforts. But if we leave the outcome to the Lord, then what do we have to fear by giving it our best shot? Think about how freeing that is. Failure does not have to be the destination. What if it is simply part of the path you are walking on as you come closer and closer to Jesus?

Jesus is the Lord of the outcome, my friend. He always has been, always will be. Say that a few times: "Jesus is the Lord of the outcome."

Moving Forward

As I was sharing with you earlier, I struggled with this fear of failure immensely. I had to face this mindset head on and be willing to "fail" if it meant I kept moving forward. Through this process I was able to see more clearly that "failure" truly is part of the process; and, as such, it is not really failure at all.

I have come to believe that true success or failure is not measured merely by the results of our first attempt at something (or even our second or third attempts). The attempt itself is a success even if the results may vary. Why do I say that? Because of the path I am walking on to get to Jesus. Sometimes I am sinking; sometimes I am walking on water. But every time I cry, "Jesus, help!" He is right there to pull me up, and I learn something new that I did not know before.

Friend, failure is not your identity. When people look at you, they do not see a blinking red sign on your forehead that reads *Failure*. Don't allow the enemy to trick you into believing that, when you make mistakes, you are branded for life. Quite the contrary, your greatest success was in choosing to surrender your life to Jesus. Now His blood washes you clean. Your every failure—past, present and future—is forever covered under His blood.

As you continue along the journey with Him, remember, failure is not the destination; it is merely part of the process. Glean from it the valuable lessons you are to learn, and rejoice.

Believe What God Says about You

God has not given us a spirit of fear, but of power and of love
and of a sound mind.

2 Timothy 1:7 NKJV

Jesus Says: Your simple obedience is success.

Declare It: I will not fear failure; I will rejoice in the lessons
learned along the way.

Apply It: Write down the areas in which you have feared failing.
What outcome were you worried about? What results were you
trying to avoid? Now grab your red pen and write next to each
item, "Jesus is Lord of the outcome."

Prayer
*Father, help me embrace this new outlook on what I con-
sider failure to be. Help me see it as part of the process
rather than a place I dread ending up. Failure is not my
identity; it is simply part of the journey I am on, and I
am ready to learn the lessons You want to teach me. Remove my fear of failure with joy for the journey. In Jesus'
mighty name. Amen.*

6

I Don't Want to Ruffle Any Feathers

IN THE SPIRIT OF HONESTY, let me get this out in the open right away: I tiptoed around people for too many years of my life, friend, and it was exhausting! There were days when I would think, *I don't know how much longer I can keep this up.* This way of life, or mode of operation (MO), became hardwired in me at an early age. Later it became my "go-to" solution when situations seemed to be getting out of control.

So I have learned much about the wall of people pleasing (also known as the fear of man) and can testify joyfully that I have seen it shatter to the ground. It no longer holds me back, and I walk in a lot of freedom these days. But it has been quite the journey, and I can slip back into this mindset if I am not careful.

It started when I was just a girl. My dad and mom divorced when I was eight. As an only child and daddy's girl (which I still am), I missed being able to spend every waking second with him. A few years later my dad remarried; and at thirteen I decided to live with him full time rather than see him only every other weekend.

After a while I found myself working overtime to prove myself. For some reason I had built up a fear that if I were not the perfect daughter, something bad might happen. And as an only child, I did not know how to integrate into a new home. I was young and did my best to adjust to the new environment. But I put an unnecessary burden on my shoulders that I needed to do everything I could to stay out of people's way and keep the peace so I would not be the cause of any discussion or, God forbid, disagreement. It was as though I tried to become invisible. *Don't worry about me. I just live here but I won't get in the way. . . .*

My dad never made me feel this way, but somehow, being a natural peacemaker, I slipped into this behavior. This was a lie the enemy whispered into my ear when I was a very young child—*Krissy, now you're just in the way*—as my mom remarried and, shortly after, so did my dad. Perhaps it had to do with the fact that I was so young when my parents divorced. Nonetheless this time period is when the mindset of *I don't want to ruffle any feathers* began for me.

As the years went on, I carried this mindset into my friendships, my career, even my marriage. I did everything I could to avoid confrontation, and bottled up my feelings because I did not want them to inconvenience anyone.

Living this way is not sustainable. It prevents people from truly coming into your world. You fear letting them in because you might let them down. You fear their seeing the real you, so you never really allow them to. Your life revolves around making everyone else happy so that people never really get to know you—the real you.

Ick! Just reflecting on this brings tears to my eyes. What a sad way to live. Yet many do live this way—myself included, for many years.

If you are dealing with this right now, my friend, be encouraged. There is much hope. The wall of people pleasing will shatter to the ground.

The Wall: People Pleasing

We are calling this wall what it is—people pleasing. It is awful and makes us afraid all the time, not to mention that it is an exhausting way to live.

The dictionary defines *people pleaser* as "a person with an emotional need to please others, often at the expense of his or her own needs or desires." People pleasers take the biblical principle of preferring others to an extreme and struggle to value and love themselves. The root of this mindset is fear, and the outcome is feeling "I'm afraid" all the time. Our inner dialogue sounds a lot like this:

- I like everyone to be happy.
- I don't want to hurt their feelings.
- What if I offend someone?
- I'd rather feel bad myself than risk making anyone else feel bad. I'll get over it.
- I don't want to get in the way.
- I don't want to ruffle any feathers.
- I don't like confrontation.

While these individual concerns can be valid, if they are out of balance, the enemy will use this inner dialogue to keep us trapped behind the wall, unable to move forward. Each statement, perpetuated over time, contributes to the structure of the wall. Before we know it, we bump up against this force every time we attempt to make progress. Our mindset becomes: *I don't want to ruffle any feathers, so I'll just hang back and let others lead the way.*

What a toll this takes on you!—not only emotionally but physically, too. The amount of stress people pleasing causes is enough to make you shut down completely if you are not careful. It is crucial that you give yourself permission to end the cycle of stuffing down your feelings and stop squelching your emotions to avoid confrontation. There are times when it is necessary for you to communicate your feelings and ruffle some feathers.

Friend, I have a question for you. Who do you think is the enemy's target with this wall? Is it the timid? The weak? Or could his target be the strong, the bold, the pioneer, the trailblazer, the trend-setter, the person God has marked to make an impact for His Kingdom here on the earth? If we get caught up in not making a dent, we will never make the difference we are called to make.

Don't let this be you, my friend. You are called to make a difference!

The Trap

The trap is set as you buy into the lie that "I am in the way." People pleasing is the enemy's way of keeping the bold timid and keeping the pioneers from blazing a trail. He wants you bound in the lie that you are less than other people. Think about it. How can I move forward in my life if I worry about getting in other people's way and, God forbid, create any waves?

Once again, the issue lies with emphasizing others' opinions over what God thinks. We put too much weight on the people around us when we need to reallocate that weight to walking out the plan God has for us here on the earth.

You are a citizen of heaven (see Philippians 3:20) but you have an important purpose on earth. Plain and simple, you need to make that difference while you can.

The Wall Shatters

The wall shatters when you believe your value in the Lord. You are not in the way. And your voice matters. God calls you "accepted in the Beloved" (Ephesians 1:6 NKJV) and His "chosen treasure" (1 Peter 2:9 TPT). God values you so deeply that He created you for this very time in His-story. He has plans for you, my friend. And His plans are good.

> "I know the plans I have for you," declares the LORD, "plans to prosper you and not to harm you, plans to give you hope and a future."
>
> Jeremiah 29:11

There are Bible stories we can pull from, like that of Moses, when the character struggled with the same things we struggle with. Then there are stories when the individual got it right. That is the case with the apostle Paul. Does that mean he never struggled with any of the same mindsets we struggle with? I suspect not. What it does mean is that, from his approach, we get a real-life example of the outcome versus the approach we ourselves often take.

Paul says this in Galatians 1:10 (TPT) about people pleasing:

> I'm obviously not trying to flatter you or water down my message to be popular with men, but my supreme passion is to please God. For if all I attempt to do is please people, I would fail to be a true servant of Christ.

Paul learned that whether he ruffled feathers or not was not the focus. His focus was on what God said about Paul, and on proceeding in obedience to Jesus' call. He laid down his need to be liked in order to follow wholly after God:

> I have been crucified with Christ and I no longer live, but Christ lives in me. The life I now live in the body, I live by faith in the Son of God, who loved me and gave himself for me.
>
> Galatians 2:20

But the enemy uses the fear of man—people pleasing—to keep us stuck behind the wall of fear so we never move forward into all that God has for us—and all that God has in store for His Kingdom on the earth through us. It is a divine partnership, us and Him. We need not fear getting in anyone's way or ruffling any feathers.

The reality is, my friend, you are going to ruffle some feathers along the way and that is okay. Think about how terrified the enemy is that you will ruffle *his* feathers and get in *his* way and hinder *his* agenda. Now can you see why he has contributed to this lie so you would form this mindset and remain stuck behind the wall of people pleasing?

But not anymore! Proverbs 29:25 (NLT) says, "Fearing people is a dangerous trap, but trusting the Lord means safety." When you trust God, you are the safest you will ever be. Even if it makes no sense. Even if you cannot see the end from the beginning. You don't have to fear ruffling feathers anymore. It is time for the daughters of God to rise in boldness and say goodbye to the timidity that often holds them back.

There is nothing wrong with you. You are not in the way. You are right where you are meant to be. Period.

Now Is the Time

I love the story of Esther. Her people, the Jews, were in danger
of being massacred by the Persians, led by their wicked enemy
in the king's court. She wanted to appeal to her husband, the
king. But she feared she would ruffle his feathers by approaching him when he had not called for her—which would mean,
since he was the king and this was the law, death. Full of fear,
Esther explained this to her cousin, Mordecai.

> "All the king's officials and the people of the royal provinces
> know that for any man or woman who approaches the king
> in the inner court without being summoned the king has but
> one law: that they be put to death unless the king extends the
> gold scepter to them and spares their lives. But thirty days have
> passed since I was called to go to the king."
>
> Esther 4:11

Her cousin's response was timeless. He asked her, in essence,
"If you don't speak now, what do you suppose you will miss
out on?" He said,

> "Do not think that because you are in the king's house you
> alone of all the Jews will escape. For if you remain silent at this
> time, relief and deliverance for the Jews will arise from another
> place, but you and your father's family will perish. And who
> knows but that you have come to your royal position for such
> a time as this?"
>
> Esther 4:13–14

Esther is known for her bravery in approaching the king
when he had not called for her and risking her life. She is known
for rising to the call on her life "for such a time as this," to
save the lives of the Jews in the kingdom. But she had not

known she would be used in such a way. She had stumbled on a moment when courage was needed. Had she succumbed to people pleasing, fearing to ruffle the feathers of her husband, the Persian king, imagine how different her story, and the lives of many Jews, would have been.

But Esther recognized the call of God on her life and that terrifying moment when she was called to action.

Friend, you, too, have a call on your life. God says, "You are My champion." Don't fear ruffling feathers if it means you are responding to His call. Don't hang back and wait for someone else to blaze the trail He is calling you to pioneer. Blaze it! Light it up. Go for it. Respond to what God says about you rather than to what your fears are saying.

My dad has an awesome "most-most" theory that he often shares: "You'll never please all the people all the time. The best you can hope for in any given scenario is 'most-most.'" He goes on to explain that not only can we not please all the people all the time, but we cannot even please all the people *most* of the time. On the people-pleasing spectrum, if you will, here is what is attainable:

- Most of the people *some* of the time.
- Some of the people *most* of the time.
- *Most* of the people *most* of the time.

Even this last, your best-case scenario—pleasing most people most of the time—takes a lot of work. It is a realistic goal, but a high one at that, and the absolute best we can ever strive for.

The point is, we may as well stop spinning our tires trying to please everyone all the time because it is not going to happen. So let's step off the hamster wheel of people pleasing. Jesus is shattering this wall today, my friend.

Moving Forward

The enemy wants to keep you stuck behind the wall of people pleasing or the fear of man. Why? You know the answer by now—to keep you from moving forward, and to keep you from seeing the Kingdom of God advancing on the earth.

My friend, it is time for this wall of people pleasing—also known as the fear of man—to shatter to the ground. Paul says, "Our purpose is to please God, not people. He alone examines the motives of our hearts" (1 Thessalonians 2:4 NLT).

Throughout my life I have experienced many seasons when I focused too much on pleasing others. In the long run this behavior never helped anyone, certainly not me, and not even those I was trying hard to please. In fact, my being inauthentic actually prolonged issues, invited a ton of unnecessary stress (on all parties) and made things messier than they needed to be. Why? Because, whether in a work environment, personal environment or somewhere else, what I was doing was not a good fit. It was kind of like an experiment with faulty data, and the faulty data was me. I was faulty because I was not being me.

I have learned much over the years. One of the most valuable lessons is to embrace who God made me to be. Willing to learn and grow, yes. But no longer willing to hide behind the fear of man, but bringing that wall to the ground so I can continue to move forward, full of faith, believing what God says about me.

I encourage you to do the same. Ruffle those feathers. Get in the way. Be beautifully you and stop worrying so much about what anyone else thinks. Acknowledge that you really do have something awesome to bring to the table: *yourself*. Give it a try, my friend. What do you have to lose? God thinks you are pretty amazing.

The wall is shattering. Can you hear it?

Believe What God Says about You

You are God's chosen treasure—priests who are kings, a spiritual "nation" set apart as God's devoted ones.

1 Peter 2:9 TPT

Jesus Says: You don't need to please others. Look to Me.

Declare It: I will focus on pleasing God, not people.

Apply It: Write down the areas where you know you have been hiding. Be bold and write the names of the people who have intimidated you. Circle each name with your red pen and write next to it, "Jesus loves you and so do I." This way you put them on a more even playing field with yourself. Each one is a person, just like you, whom Jesus loves and whom you don't need worry so much about pleasing.

Prayer
Father, help me put less emphasis on what other people think of me and more emphasis on how You feel about me. Cause me to grow in value based on what You say about me. You say I am loved. You say I am set apart and chosen. Thank You for Your love. In Jesus' name. Amen.

PART 3

I'm Overwhelmed

Definition of *overwhelm*

1. To affect someone very strongly.
2. To cause someone to have too many things to deal with.
3. To defeat someone or something completely.

Mindsets

1. I'm so overwhelmed.
2. I'm not good at saying no.
3. I'm all alone.

Walls

1. Overwhelm
2. Being stretched too thin
3. Loneliness

7

I'm So Overwhelmed

OVERWHELM. Need I say more?

Even as I write this chapter, my husband is home sick from work after five days of having a cough. We are still awaiting the results of his Covid test because the lab is backed up, which means our kids are missing school and all their activities for the week. I am on a tight deadline to finish this book and am doing my best to juggle the day-to-day as well as the anomalies of the week, such as notifying teachers and coaches. I am doing my very best to hold myself together, but it is tough.

As women we can all relate to the feeling of being overwhelmed. We stretch ourselves too thin; we try to keep up with the expectations and demands of our day-to-day lives; and we often get super lonely in the process. We are taking care of everything and everyone around us when our heavenly Father is looking at us, saying, *Daughter, don't forget to take care of yourself as well*. But how do we do that?

One of the reasons we get overwhelmed is because we do not seem to stop. We run and run and run (sometimes literally) and have a difficult time stopping to rest. Sound familiar? We pay little attention to our limits, and before we know it, we are overwhelmed, burned out and just plain done. Our energy is zapped and we are not sure how to proceed. The overwhelm is just too much.

While becoming overwhelmed from time to time is normal, it can, if we are not careful, become our lifestyle. We can get used to feeling that way and almost crave the chaos in order to continue forward. At that point overwhelm becomes a wall, hindering us from making the progress Father God wants us to make, and we are not always aware that the wall even exists. We just know there is something stopping us and keeping us—well, overwhelmed.

Because of the nature of overwhelm, when we face this wall, we often feel incapable of moving forward. It is too much to think about, and we are not only convinced we will remain here long term, but we feel almost justified in remaining here, simply because of how overwhelmed we really are.

My friend, how long you stay behind this wall is really up to you. I wish I had better news. But if you think about it, that *is* good news . . . because it means there is something you can do about it. You are not helpless or hopeless. You can grab onto Jesus today and see that wall of overwhelm shatter to the ground.

The Wall: Overwhelm

Overwhelm is defined as "affecting someone very strongly; causing someone to have too many things to deal with; or defeating someone or something completely."

Overwhelm is the enemy's tactic meant to overtake you completely, so you feel defeated, stuck and wanting to quit. It causes you to stay where you are, unable to move forward into the plans

God has for you. You make choices you would not normally make, such as giving up too soon, disconnecting with someone you love, suffering in your performance at work, or being less patient with your kids.

Overwhelm caused

- Peter to deny Christ;
- Jonah to want to die;
- Elijah to hide and give up;
- Esther to fast and pray so she could do the impossible;
- Jesus to cry out to God in the Garden of Gethsemane.

Overwhelm affects each of us uniquely, but as you can see from the above list, when we shift our focus onto what God can do, overwhelm can have a positive impact on our lives.

There are many causes of overwhelm: stress, anxiety, traumatic experiences, work, the unexpected, and many more. While it is often associated with circumstances—either multiple small things piling up or one or two big events that occur suddenly—it is also linked to a person's individual capacity to cope. Below are some environmental stressors we can all relate to:

- work responsibilities
- relationship problems
- traumatic experiences
- financial worries
- political issues
- environmental warnings
- health concerns
- living in a global pandemic

Some people are more inclined than others to become over-whelmed. I am one of those who can do many things at one time, but who can become overwhelmed pretty quickly if I am not careful—like when things compound or when I am pulled in multiple directions by external forces (such as my kids or people in my life). As an introvert, I have to learn my limits and make sure I am taking time to regroup and strategize how I handle the juggling.

A key has been compartmentalizing tasks to certain hours of the day. This has been a game changer for me. I address certain items at certain times, making sure to maximize the times and days my kiddos are in school. When those times are over, I don't think about it again until the next scheduled time. This works well—until suddenly my kids are home sick from school; my husband is home sick from work waiting on a backed-up lab for the results of a Covid test; I have to provide a play-by-play of the daily update to multiple teachers and coaches; and I am dealing with an impending writing deadline that I cannot extend.

Okay, now I am sweating! But it really is okay. Ha! I just have to remember my protocol: Stop, breathe and pray. (I share more about this in just a bit.)

The Trap

The trap is set as the enemy convinces you that all hope is gone and you are defeated. He causes you to believe that tending to your emotional well-being is selfish. He overwhelms you with doubt, worry and a conviction that you will never overcome.

Each one of us has our own capacity. Learning yours is a major key in overcoming overwhelm. The good news is that Jesus will help you with this.

Jonah was so overwhelmed that he ran from the Lord.

The word of the LORD came to Jonah son of Amittai: "Go to the great city of Nineveh and preach against it, because its wickedness has come up before me." But Jonah ran away from the LORD and headed for Tarshish. He went down to Joppa, where he found a ship bound for that port. After paying the fare, he went aboard and sailed for Tarshish to flee from the LORD.

Jonah 1:1–3

Peter was so overwhelmed by the circumstances around him during the time Jesus was on trial that he did the unthinkable: He denied Christ. We looked at that terrible scene in chapter 2. He did the very thing he assured Jesus he would never do, and "he went outside and wept bitterly" (Luke 22:62).

Overwhelm causes us to do the unthinkable, doesn't it? This is why the enemy loves this trap. His agenda is to steal, kill and destroy, and when we are overwhelmed, it makes his job a lot easier.

But it doesn't have, to my friend—as always, because of Jesus. We have so much hope!

The Wall Shatters

The wall shatters as we run to the feet of Jesus, casting all our cares on Him, and leaving them there. Jesus extends this invitation: "Come to me, all you who are weary and burdened, and I will give you rest" (Matthew 11:28). I love this portion of Scripture in *The Message* translation:

> "Are you tired? Worn out? Burned out on religion? Come to me. Get away with me and you'll recover your life. I'll show you how to take a real rest. Walk with me and work with me—watch how I do it. Learn the unforced rhythms of grace. I won't lay

anything heavy or ill-fitting on you. Keep company with me and you'll learn to live freely and lightly."

verses 28–30

How often do you feel as though your whole life is out of control? We often wonder what we even do with this mess of a life we find ourselves in. How did we get here and how do we move forward? Jesus offers clear instruction in this passage on how we can recover our life, and it is by tucking away with Him: "Get away with me and you'll recover your life." We find our refuge and strength in Him.

Overwhelmed? Jesus says, "I'll show you how to take a real rest. Walk with me and work with me—watch how I do it." How remarkable is this? We are invited to walk with Him and even work with Him and through Him. This leads us into those "unforced rhythms of grace." Jesus says He won't give us anything heavy to carry. His promise is for us to continue moving forward with Him and through Him, living free and light.

Acts 17:28 says, "In him we live and move and have our being." How beautiful that we have this gift available to us!

The problem is, are you utilizing this divine resource in your day-to-day life—living and moving and having your being in Him? I suspect not, at least not always; but that is okay, because you will now, my friend, as you say goodbye to the overwhelm that has been holding you back and move into the "unforced rhythms of grace" propelling you forward.

Sometimes I have to say to myself, *Krissy, just stop. Breathe. And pray.* It reminds me of the emergency response I was taught in elementary school of what to do in case of fire: "Stop, drop and roll." I think we need the same kind of knee-jerk protocol built in as we deal with overwhelm. Since the nature of overwhelm is to prevent us from thinking calmly and rationally, we need to initiate the self-talk response: *Stop, breathe and pray.* When we do, we enter those unforced rhythms of grace, and we experience Jesus' love and peace washing over us, giving us fresh perspective.

This pulls us out of the stress response to overwhelm and into the divine order of Jesus when we remember, *Oh, yeah—God's got this.* And the wall shatters to the ground.

Moving Forward

It is important that we see in the pages of New Testament the power of the Holy Spirit in operation inside us, preventing overwhelm from overtaking us.

Look at Jesus. He was overwhelmed with the burden of the cross, which led Him to cry out to God. The apostles were overwhelmed with risking their lives to preach the Gospel, but they kept going, and writing that they were filled with hope, peace and joy because of the power of the Holy Spirit in them.

You have this same help, my friend. Draw on the power of God so you continue moving forward and see the wall of overwhelm shatter to the ground.

Let's review some of the instructions the apostle Paul gave the Philippian believers. He knew a thing or two about overwhelm. The following is from The Passion Translation:

> Don't be pulled in different directions or worried about a thing. Be saturated in prayer throughout each day, offering your faith-filled requests before God with overflowing gratitude. Tell him every detail of your life, then God's wonderful peace that transcends human understanding, will guard your heart and mind through Jesus Christ. Keep your thoughts continually fixed on all that is authentic and real, honorable and admirable, beautiful and respectful, pure and holy, merciful and kind. And fasten

your thoughts on every glorious work of God, praising him
always.

Philippians 4:6–8 TPT

We could pause long and hard on just the first sentence:
"Don't be pulled in different directions or worried about a thing"
(verse 6). Easier said than done, right? Especially for women. If
only! But this addresses our faith walk, our inner compass that
can sway our faith to the right or to the left. Paul's instruction
is meant to keep us anchored in Christ Jesus.

Paul goes on, "Be saturated in prayer throughout each day"
(verse 6). This is a major key to moving forward—to overwhelm
our overwhelm with prayer. We posture ourselves as vessels
needing daily filling and refreshing in the presence of God. We
say, "I need You, Jesus." From this place we make our requests
known unto God, which causes an overflow effect within of
gratitude. What a beautiful image! I am feeling a calming effect
even now as I write these words. God's peace overwhelms us,
friend—His "wonderful peace that transcends human understanding" (verse 7).

What happens next is the ripple effect of our pausing in
His presence. His peace becomes a shield guarding our hearts
and minds through Jesus. His peace calms us. His peace pro-
tects our hearts from the side effects of overwhelm. Stress and
anxiety are washed away by His cascading peace in our hearts
and minds.

Then Paul instructs us on what to do with our thought life:

Keep your thoughts continually fixed on all that is authentic
and real, honorable and admirable, beautiful and respectful,
pure and holy, merciful and kind. And fasten your thoughts on
every glorious work of God, praising him always.

verse 8 TPT

This reminds me of David's words:

Gaze upon him, join your life with his, and joy will come. Your faces will glisten with glory. You'll never wear that shame-face again. When I had nothing, desperate and defeated, I cried out to the Lord and he heard me, bringing his miracle-deliverance when I needed it most.

Psalm 34:5–6 TPT

A shift occurs when we focus our minds on Jesus. Paul says to focus "on all that is authentic and real." What could that be other than God's Word and His promises? When you are feeling overwhelmed, think about what God has spoken to and over you. Think about the bigness of God. He has no limits. He promises to rescue you whenever you are feeling overwhelmed.

When holy lovers of God cry out to him with all their hearts, the Lord will hear them and come to rescue them from all their troubles. The Lord is close to all whose hearts are crushed by pain, and he is always ready to restore the repentant one. Even when bad things happen to the good and godly ones, the Lord will save them and not let them be defeated by what they face.

Psalm 34:17–19 TPT

Believe What God Says about You

Whenever my busy thoughts were out of control, the soothing comfort of your presence calmed me down and overwhelmed me with delight.

Psalm 94:19 TPT

Jesus Says: Come to Me. I will give you rest.

Declare It: I will overwhelm the overwhelm with prayer.

Apply It: Write down the areas in which you experience the most overwhelm. Write down some of the known triggers for overwhelm as you get more and more familiar with your personal capacity. What are some protocols you can put into place to ensure that you "stop, breathe and pray" as a first response to stress and worry? Most importantly, what is God saying to you?

Prayer

Father, overwhelm me with Your love. Wash me with Your peace. Let Your love cascade over my heart and mind as I focus on Your faithfulness. Prepare my heart as I move forward into this next section on overwhelm. Shatter each wall, in Jesus' mighty name.

8

I'm Not Good at Saying No

"HI, I'M KRISSY. I'm notorious for juggling multiple tasks and projects at one time."

Can you relate, by any chance? I know many can. Over the years I have worked hard to find a good balance for the many passion projects I have pursued. It has taken a long time, but now, finally, I feel I have landed on a good method. I have been able to assign each project its own season and timeline. Across the span of a year, there is not too much overlap. Among my books, my show and my courses, I am able to alternate my focus on each of these, one at a time.

This is secondary, of course, to being a wife and mom. But now that both of my kids are in school, I have a pretty good routine established between the hours I drop them off and pick them up.

Sounds nice, huh? Well, let me assure you, this has not always been the case. In fact, up until recently, I only dreamed of being able to share what I just shared.

Prior to the global pandemic beginning in 2020, I had a pretty good rhythm going with my schedule and family life. It seemed I was finally finding a groove. Then March 2020 hit, and all that went down the drain. The day was March 15, 2020, in the week prior to the world shutting down. (I feel as if I am about to write a dramatic screenplay or something. Ha ha! But that is not too far off, is it?)

Anyway, that week Donovan and the kids and I had just moved out of our home and into my grandparents' home. We were in the process of relocating our family of four to another state. Just as we were just settling into our temporary dwelling, the pandemic threatened the health and safety of the entire world, and everything began to shut down. Businesses closed. Schools transitioned to remote learning. It was pure chaos. You probably remember very well.

Needless to say, a wrench was thrown into the delicate stability I had worked so hard to establish. That is when the "pretty good rhythm" I mentioned earlier began to unravel. All my passion projects went on hold until further notice—meaning I had no clue when I would be able to resume my focus on them. My newest book was scheduled to release in just a few months, but all the media surrounding it . . . well, who knew what that would look like with airlines cutting flights and with social distancing in full effect? We had to postpone launching the new season of my show indefinitely due to the uncertainty. And I had just begun helping with a business start-up; those plans were also affected. My kids—oh, my sweet, amazing kids!—well, they, like many others, had to be homeschooled.

To call this an overwhelming season is quite the understatement, and at this point it was only beginning.

Our move ended up delayed, and we lived with my grandparents for nine months, essentially during the height of the early pandemic. Since my grandparents were in their mid-80s, I lived in constant fear that I was going to get them sick. Eventually we began the process of having a new home built, which took a few months longer than expected. At times we were not even sure we were going to be able to close on it, due to a myriad of twists and turns along the way. And somewhere in there I launched that new book as well.

It all seems like a blur. I was doing multiple remote media interviews for the launch of my book, many of them over the phone or via Zoom, sitting in my car, because the kids were inside being, well, kids. We were still homeschooling, still living with grandparents, still unsure when we would be able to move.

Please allow me to clarify. I am not complaining about my life! I realize how very blessed we are, and I am thankful none of us got sick during that time, especially my amazing, Jesus-loving grandparents, who let the four of us live with them for nine whole months! When I tell you I have learned what it means to put family first and be a "giver" from my grandparents, I am not kidding. They are the most generous, sacrificial people I have ever known, and I am honored to call them my family. During this time, I was able to see God's hand on their lives and was challenged by their steadfast prayer lives and faith walk.

Nonetheless all this led up to a bottleneck of the projects I had in motion—which occurred the following year.

We moved into our new home in our new state just in time to ring in the new year. With all my major projects delayed due to Covid and homeschooling, they ended up on the same time-table. Whereas I had carefully crafted a seasonal schedule for each one, now they all demanded the same level of focus at the same time. I needed to be five different people at one time—one for my kids and homeschooling; one to work on my new book;

one for my show; one for a new digital course I was writing; and one just to help the other four. I thought I was going to burst. I did not want to let anyone down, so I tried to hang on tightly to each item and give it my best—but oh my, I felt as if I were failing in every area.

This went on for too long—a few months, really—until I could hardly take it anymore. I had moved from stress to distress. Not good.

I will never forget waking up in sheer panic at two o'clock one morning. My head was spinning. I was short of breath, and it felt as if my lungs were collapsing. I slipped out of bed and made my way to my cozy little den at the front of our new home, careful not to make a peep and wake any of my sleeping family.

I snuggled in with a blanket and a cup of chamomile tea and sobbed quietly. Tears spilled from my eyes like rivers that had been pent up by a dam. You know that silent, ugly cry when your entire body travails, snot is flying, tears are streaming, but no sound is coming out of you, because if it did, you might blow the roof off the house and wake the neighborhood with your cries? Well, that was me in the wee hours of that morning.

"I just can't do this, Lord," I whispered. "I feel like I need to quit everything. I can't take this level of stress anymore. Should I just walk away from it all? I can't see any other way."

I felt like a rubber band that had been stretched to the breaking point, and at any moment, with the slightest amount of additional pressure, I would snap.

Did I need to say no to things I had already given my yes to? Did I need to go to a professional counselor? The answer was unclear to me. All I knew was that I felt fragile and needed Jesus desperately.

The thing with saying yes too often and not saying no when you should is that you will end up feeling stretched too thin.

And at this point, the people in your life do not always realize how stretched you really are. Not that you want them to. God forbid that people have to walk on eggshells around you. But if someone, anyone, could have some sort of super-hero goggles that could see straight through the "I'm fine" smile you put on during the day, and see just how fragile you really are—you think it might help.

You know that feeling when everything compounds? You worry over things you would not normally worry over. That was me at two in the morning. Suddenly I found myself concerned over our finances, my husband's job, my kids' education. I even ventured so far into the future as to be concerned over their colleges. Would they still get into good schools after having me as their teacher during these formative years in their early childhood development? If I walked away from everything causing me stress, how would we even afford college? And my dog—what would I do with my dog? What about her?

What was wrong with my dog? Well, nothing, but I sure did worry about her—just because. Because I was stretched. Stretched to a limit to which I had not been stretched before.

So there I sat, alone in the dark in my cozy little den, wrapped in a blanket, sobbing silently. I sobbed and sobbed. Just when I did not think I could cry anymore, I did.

But then I began to pray. I poured out my cares and concerns and issues at the feet of Jesus that morning. Eventually I became calm. And you know something? I felt a sense of relief. I think the crying helped. Or was it the praying? I am sure both. The more I cried, the more I released the burden I had been carrying onto Jesus. Finally! And the more I cast my cares onto the Lord, the more He helped me. He is so good that way.

Jesus says, "Come to me, all you who are weary and burdened, and I will give you rest" (Matthew 11:28). And come to Him I did. As I prayed and sought the Lord for help, He gave me wisdom and strategy on how to move forward. Pen and paper in hand, I began to write down His instructions as to how I could reorganize my life to individual seasons all over again, to ensure the dedicated focus that each deserved. You know what else Jesus showed me? Things I needed to let go of completely—areas in which I needed to say no.

Talk about your life-changing two a.m. encounter with Jesus! When I had slammed right into the wall of being stretched too thin, Jesus shattered the wall and showed me how to keep moving forward.

The Wall: Being Stretched Too Thin

The dictionary defines *being stretched* as "being amplified or enlarged beyond natural or proper limits."

If we have a difficult time saying no, we can easily become stretched too thin, which makes us feel overwhelmed. By definition, if we are stretched too thin, we have not only reached our natural or proper limit, but we have gone beyond it. If we live our lives always at max capacity, we never really move forward. Even though we feel we are working and doing and moving and juggling, we are not really making progress. We have no real momentum. We are, in fact, spinning our tires.

Some outcomes to being stretched too thin are:

- We quit.
- We compromise.
- We sacrifice the "peace pace." More about this in a minute.
- We crash and burn.

If you are feeling stretched too thin, my friend, you may have too much on your plate. Or some restructuring is in order.

Either way, it is time to sit with the Lord before you crash and seek Him for wisdom. Ask Him:

- Do I have too much on my plate?
- Do I need to reorganize my life?

Simply sit and wait on Him. Listen as He speaks. Don't fear the direction He may offer, as it is always for your benefit and well-being.

Here are some important items to note about what saying no is and is not:

- Saying no is not quitting.
- Saying no is not compromising.
- Saying no is saying yes to less stress.
- Saying no creates opportunities to say yes to the right things.

Experiencing some level of stress is normal and even okay, as it causes increased alertness and focus. Stress can be motivating as it creates excitement, enthusiasm and even sharpness to address the immediate situation. If you are stressed over a test you have prepared for, you have sharpened alertness as you take it. Brides who plan their weddings for months experience stress from the many details, yet excitement for the special day.

What you want to be concerned about is *distress*. When our stress moves into overwhelm, then we are in distress, which is counterproductive, an indicator that you have taken on too much. You will know the difference because normal, healthy stress carries with it excitement and motivation, while distress carries with it a sense of overwhelm that can lead to discouragement, anxiety, a desire to give up, and potentially an emotional breakdown.

Don't sacrifice your peace for the sake of being busy or trying to achieve more than you have the capacity for in any given season.

Over the years I have had to learn the "peace pace"—something my dad taught me when I shared with him my aspirations, dreams and the inner drive I have to keep moving forward, to continue creating and teaching and building. Dad would say, "This is all good, Krissy. Just be sure you're going at a peace pace." I have come to recognize the peace pace as momentum without stress—our ability to continue moving forward without sacrificing our peace.

The Trap

The trap is set when we have a false sense of accomplishment because of all our busyness, and we fear saying no because we might let someone down. It may take us a while to realize we are not really moving forward. Meanwhile the enemy is happy because he has managed to halt our progress, and because he has us in the vicious cycle of stress, worry, busyness and overwhelm.

But this is not where it ends for us, my friend. In fact, this is a beautiful beginning—right in the place of overwhelm. Why do I say that? Because what better time than when we are overwhelmed to throw it all at the feet of Jesus, casting our cares on Him once and for all and leaving them all there?

Let's face it. When we feel stretched too thin, we want to quit. Give up. Throw in the towel. How can we possibly move forward, especially when we feel we have nothing left to give?

When I arrived at this breaking point, I asked myself, *How did I get here? How did I allow myself to become stretched so thin?* I knew in my heart my motivation for working so hard was to provide for my family. But I wondered, was I being overly ambitious? And is it a bad thing to stretch yourself and push boundaries and limits?

Two good questions. The answers are found in two other questions: *What is God asking of you? And what has He put on your plate?*

You may answer those questions by saying you are confident that all the projects or tasks you have taken on, you heard from the Lord. Or you may be going, *I haven't asked for any of this. I have no choice—I'm a career woman [or a working mom] and doing my best simply to juggle life's day-to-day demands.*

No matter the scenario, the sensation of being stretched too thin can build the wall of overwhelm, hindering us from moving forward. What is the pathway from here?

The Wall Shatters

The wall shatters when we pour it all out at Jesus' feet. All our ambitions, all our overwhelm, all our stress, all our anxiety. The wall shatters, friend, when we release our cares onto Jesus. Like the woman washing Jesus' feet with her tears, she forsook it all just to reach Him. Once she was there, she wept at His feet, kissing them, wetting them with her tears, wiping them with her hair and pouring perfume on them. You can read the story in Luke 7:36–50. Scripture says she had "lived a sinful life" (verse 37). I don't know what all she had been through, but her mannerisms suggest that she was overwhelmed. And thankfully she found the One worthy of her tears.

Not learning to say no can turn our focus from the simplicity of sitting at Jesus' feet, as she did.

Our souls can grow weary, so the Bible instructs us to guard our hearts and be careful about the welfare of our souls.

Above all, guard the affections of your heart, for they affect all that you are. Pay attention to the welfare of your innermost being, for from there flows the wellspring of life.

Proverbs 4:23 TPT

Some of Jesus' final words before His crucifixion also describe the kind of life we can live as His followers. He said, "I am leaving you with a gift—peace of mind and heart. And the peace I give is a gift the world cannot give. So don't be troubled or afraid" (John 14:27 NLT). Imagine living your life full of this gift of peace. Is it even possible? How do we live daily with this gift in operation?

By guarding our hearts and the welfare of our souls.

Don't take on so much, my friend. Strategize with Jesus what your day and week should look like. Organize your life to make more room for Him and more room for the things you enjoy. Yes, work hard. Yes, take the leap forward into all that God has for you. But be sure you are moving forward at a "peace pace" as you do.

It is important, friend, to give yourself grace. It is also important that you learn from when you have taken on too much, and do your best not to repeat the pattern.

Moving Forward

Make the decision to guard your time, your talents and your heart. Decide today that you will be slower to take the leap and more strategic about what you pile onto your to-do list. Ask yourself: *Is this adding value to my life? Or is this stealing my joy?* Follow the pace of peace. Remember that peace pace is momentum (i.e., progress) without stress. It comes from being like the woman washing Jesus' feet with her tears, wiping them with her hair and pouring perfume on them.

114

We can cast all our cares on Him. Trusting Him. Listening to Him. Loving Him.

By saying no to unnecessary stressors, you are saying yes to yourself. As a result, your soul will prosper and you will experience peace. What is He saying to you today? Sit with Him and strategize. He is brilliant at helping you sort out all the areas in which you have taken on too much. As you do, listen as that wall of "stretched too thin" shatters to the ground. The overwhelm will lift and you will feel His peace cover you like a warm blanket.

Can you hear that wall of being stretched too thin beginning to crack?

Believe What God Says about You

"Peace I leave with you; my peace I give you. I do not give to you as the world gives. Do not let your hearts be troubled and do not be afraid."

John 14:27

Jesus Says: I have a gift for you—My peace.

Declare It: I will say no to more so I can say yes to less stress. I will commit to prayerfully considering every opportunity or open door before giving my yes.

Apply It: Write down the areas in which you have taken on too much. List each item. Now take your red pen and ask the Lord to highlight the areas to which you need to say no or else restructure/reorganize. Ask Him to help you prioritize your list and remove anything that should not be there.

Prayer

Father, would You show me where I need to say no so I can say yes to less stress? Empower me with the courage to let go of needing to do so much all the time. Remove this burden as I cast all my cares at the feet of Jesus. Ignite me with fresh hope that I can live my life at a more peaceful pace as I move forward. In Jesus' name. Amen.

9

I'm All Alone

"I CAN'T TAKE THIS ANYMORE. I'm all alone and I need to know, God, if You are real. Where are You?"

These words, mixed with sobs, spilled out of me as my heart ached for love. I was fifteen years old and had walked with Jesus my entire life, yet I had never felt more alone than I did in this very moment.

"There has to be more," I continued. "There must be something I'm missing. I need You, God."

Here I was in a room surrounded by people yet feeling as though I were alone on a deserted island. It felt as if no one really knew me. No one understood what I was walking through and the isolation I experienced.

To be honest, it would not have mattered if they did, because I was at the point when I needed a touch from my heavenly Father more than I needed a person to assure me, "Everything is going to be okay," without really knowing for sure. I was at a breaking point and did not know how to move forward from the loneliness I had become used to.

Loneliness had become my friend—a constant companion, one that never left my side. I could count on loneliness. I could rely on it to remind me who I was—a loner, someone no one really understood, a mystery destined to be alone her whole life. *You repel the people around you*, it would say. *People always leave*, it would warn me as I began letting someone in. *Make sure you have an exit strategy* was its instruction when new friendships would emerge. I had learned this behavior over several years of people coming and going in my young life like a revolving door. My defense mechanism was now built, and loneliness was calling the shots.

So here I was, fifteen years old and at the end of my rope. I had my fleece positioned on the ground—like the fleece Gideon asked God to make first wet, then dry, to confirm His leading—and I needed God to reveal Himself to me once and for all.

And my oh my, did He ever!

I was attending a beautiful revival service at another church with some members of my family, when two people came and prayed over me, speaking life and hope to my weary soul. Suddenly I felt two hands reach down from above and push me to the floor. I found myself in a kneeling position, propped up by my trembling arms. I began to weep as the pain from the loneliness I had been living with came pouring out through my tears. My heart finally opened and I felt safe—safe to release the hurt, the misconceptions, the fears, the agony I had been experiencing.

I could feel the loneliness leaving my side, and in its place, the power and presence of almighty God. He was wrapping me up and holding me in His arms. Only with difficulty, as I tried to get up and walk, did I make my way back to my family.

My uncle looked at me and said simply, "He's big, isn't He?"

At that my knees gave way and I fell to the floor, weeping. His words resonated with what I was encountering, and I did not know it until he said them. Yes, I was experiencing the bigness and realness of God, and my physical body was unable to stand in His presence.

In the car after the service, I lay in the back listening as my heavenly Father spoke into my life. He spoke right to my soul—to the core of me—and told me who I am: *Krissy, I have always been with you, and now I have my arms wrapped around you.*

Nearly every Bible verse I had ever learned raced through my mind, coming to life. God was replacing the identity that loneliness had declared over me with His own declarations: *You are Mine. I love you. I have a plan for your life. You are not alone.* These were just some of the powerful statements washing over me, making me new.

The rest of that night I lay in bed, still wrapped up in the Father's arms, as He spoke life and hope and truth to me. I remember waking up in the dark, sitting straight up in bed and going to specific Bible passages the Lord led me to. I am not sure how I could see the words on the page except by the light of the moon and the radiance of God's presence all around me.

When I woke up the next morning, I knew for the first time in many years exactly who I was. I will never forget the fresh sense of hope I felt as I put my feet on the floor, lifted my head to look toward the heavenlies and said, "Good morning, Lord."

That encounter changed everything. From that day forward, while the circumstances in my life did not necessarily change, my mindset sure did. Jesus replaced my thought that *I'm all alone* with *I am never alone; Jesus is right here with me.* My companion, loneliness, was gone and in its place was the "friend who sticks closer than a brother" (Proverbs 18:24). Jesus. Just Jesus. He was and is always there and has never left my side.

The Wall: Loneliness

The dictionary defines *loneliness* as "being without company; cut off from others; sadness from being alone; a feeling of bleakness or desolation."

A recent study showed that 36 percent of all Americans, including 61 percent of young adults and 51 percent of mothers with young children, feel a sense of "serious loneliness."[7]

The wall of loneliness is exacerbated by a perception that everyone else around us is connected, but we are not. That feeling of being all alone can be unbearable at times. We truly wonder if there is anyone out there who can relate to what we are experiencing.

Your inner dialogue sounds a lot like this:

- No one gets me.
- I'll always be alone.
- I feel left out.
- They don't like me once they get to know me.
- I disappoint the people in my life.

Loneliness can lead to deep feelings of

- Isolation
- Depression
- Oppression

The Trap

The trap is set when we believe the lie that "everyone else is connected but I am all alone." The enemy pursues us when

7. "Loneliness in America: How the Pandemic Has Deepened an Epidemic of Loneliness and What We Can Do About It," Making Caring Common Project, Harvard Graduate School of Education, February 2021, https://mcc.gse.harvard.edu/reports/loneliness-in-america.

we are in this isolated, lonely condition. Why? Because it is here that he can deceive us into believing his lies. He assaults us with false accusations about who we are. It is in isolation that we are most susceptible to believing his lies, because when we look around or reach out for help, no one is there. And we begin to buy in.

By design, we are created as part of a whole. Each one of us is made in the image of God, and we are each a component of the Body of Christ. The Bible says we are different parts of the same body, and we all need one another. When we don't recognize this and feel disconnected from others, whether real or imagined, we may want to quit—and with no one around us, we wonder, *Who will even notice if I do?*

Elijah, a prophet of the Lord, experienced this. Let's take a look at part of his story.

In the book of 1 Kings we read about the miracles God was performing through Elijah to reveal Himself to His people. At that time Baal, the Canaanite god, was being worshiped in Israel. In fact, Baal worship was so widespread that Elijah actually thought he was all alone—the only one left in Israel serving God.

Elijah set up a competition between God and Baal, and the Lord was shown to be the one true God, causing the people to cry, "The LORD—he is God!" (1 Kings 18:39). Then Elijah executed 450 prophets of Baal. At that Jezebel was furious and put out a message to Elijah that his life was over.

Behind the scenes the enemy was appalled at the spiritual impact Elijah was having in Israel and wanted to put a stop to it. He decided to wear him down until he gave up. So when Jezebel sent word that she was going to hunt him down and take his life "by this time tomorrow" (1 Kings 19:2), the prophet of God, terrified, made a run for it.

This is where we are privy to his internal dialogue of feeling totally alone, depressed and wanting to give up. We read about his journey in 1 Kings 19 as he sat under a bush and begged the Lord to take his life.

> "I have had enough, Lord," he said. "Take my life; I am no better than my ancestors." Then he lay down under the bush and fell asleep.
>
> verses 4–5a

What happened next is powerful, my friend. We see how God was pursuing Elijah.

> All at once an angel touched him and said, "Get up and eat." He looked around, and there by his head was some bread baked over hot coals, and a jar of water. He ate and drank and then lay down again.
>
> verses 5b–6

The Lord never gives up on us. He is always there. The angel of the Lord was with Elijah, giving him food and drink to sustain him, and encouraging him to continue moving forward.

You see, Elijah thought he was running away and giving up, when really he was on an important journey, moving toward an encounter with the living God. He needed to hear afresh what God said about him and what He had for him to do.

> The angel of the Lord came back a second time and touched him and said, "Get up and eat, for the journey is too much for you." So he got up and ate and drank. Strengthened by that food, he traveled forty days and forty nights until he reached Horeb, the mountain of God. There he went into a cave and spent the night.
>
> verses 7–9a

Up next is my favorite part of the story.

> And the word of the LORD came to him: "What are you doing here, Elijah?"
>
> He replied, "I have been very zealous for the LORD God Almighty. The Israelites have rejected your covenant, torn down your altars, and put your prophets to death with the sword. I am the only one left, and now they are trying to kill me too."
>
> The LORD said, "Go out and stand on the mountain in the presence of the LORD, for the LORD is about to pass by."
>
> verses 9b–11a

This was the first time Elijah told the Lord that he was all alone, the only one left. Was he? We will see in a minute.

And do you see how the voice of the Lord instructed Elijah to "go out"? In other words, *Get up, move forward and trust that I have something for you.*

God's question to Elijah—"What are you doing here?"—leaped off the page when I read it not too long ago. I found myself in a pit and feeling quite lonely. When I read those words, I felt as though the Lord was speaking them right to my soul: *What are you doing here, Krissy?* In other words, *This is a strange place for you to be. In the pit of loneliness? Again? What are you doing here again?*

Tears streamed down my face as I heard the whisper of God speaking directly to me and right into the core of my current situation. I was working so hard and trying so hard, and in my exhaustion, I felt lost and was becoming reacquainted with my old friend loneliness.

> Then a great and powerful wind tore the mountains apart and shattered the rocks before the LORD, but the LORD was not in the wind. After the wind there was an earthquake, but the LORD

was not in the earthquake. After the earthquake came a fire, but the LORD was not in the fire. And after the fire came a gentle whisper. When Elijah heard it, he pulled his cloak over his face and went out and stood at the mouth of the cave.

Then a voice said to him, "What are you doing here, Elijah?"

He replied, "I have been very zealous for the LORD God Almighty. The Israelites have rejected your covenant, torn down your altars, and put your prophets to death with the sword. I am the only one left, and now they are trying to kill me too."

The LORD said to him, "Go back the way you came, and go to the Desert of Damascus."

1 Kings 19:11b–15

For the second time Elijah had told the Lord, "I am the only one left." He felt isolated and alone. But God told him,

"I reserve seven thousand in Israel—all whose knees have not bowed to Baal and whose mouths have not kissed him."

verse 18

Three times God asked Elijah, "What are you doing here?" Often we find ourselves in a pit of loneliness, like Elijah. When we do, it is important that we wait for that gentle, life-changing voice of the Lord. Listen as He asks you the same question: *What are you doing here?* In other words, *This is no place for you. You don't need to be in this pit. Get up and get moving.* Listen to what God says about you.

Elijah was refreshed in the presence of God and then instructed to go back to where he had come from. There was purpose for him there. He would meet and anoint Elisha, the young man who would become his apprentice and succeed him as prophet in Israel.

Friend, sometimes we just need a fresh encounter with Jesus that will change everything. We need a refreshing, a reminder that we are not alone.

The Wall Shatters

The wall shatters when we surrender, waiting on the Lord and following His instruction. As we begin to let go, we allow God to move into those lonely places and fill them up with His fresh voice of hope. Of healing. Of deliverance. We become revived in His presence. We feel alive again. We have new hope and new energy to continue moving forward.

What you may see as an end or breaking point, God sees as an opening. He loves when we get to breaking points. I know that is a little hard to hear, because to us a breaking point is that place we never want to reach. But I have learned over the years that, after carrying the load for so long on our own, this is the place where we finally let go and surrender; where we forsake it all to lay it at His feet. It is sort of our "Jesus take the wheel; I'm going all in" catalyst moment when we finally allow God to take our burdens from us and place over us His blanket of peace.

Moving Forward

I have experienced a few seasons when that old "friend" loneliness tried to come back into my life and erect the wall that had shattered to the ground all those years earlier. The only time it was successful was when I was in another uncharted, vulnerable place in my life—a place I had never been before and for which I had no roadmap. This was when I became a mom for the first time. This was a time in my life when I would have assumed I would be feeling the most surrounded. Instead I felt totally alone all over again.

I am not even sure why. Maybe it was all the hormones, the sleep deprivation, the pressure of taking care of a new life that was utterly dependent on me. Likely it was all of the above. I felt as if I was learning a brand-new language, one I did not yet have the dialect for, so trying to communicate what I was feeling typically came out in tears.

Motherhood was not what I expected at all. It was more difficult and more amazing, in equal portions, than I could ever have imagined. I never felt like more of a success and more of a failure both at once than in those early days of being a mom for the first time. And this went on for many, many months.

I began to feel all over again that no one understood me, as though the needs I had were ridiculous, so I stopped expressing them. This led me to yet another season of feeling isolated. I was still working, and as I mentioned earlier in this book, I found myself no longer desiring the same things I had desired pre-motherhood. My ambitions had all changed. I had changed. Everything had changed.

It was in this place that that old companion loneliness got to work on the wall, and before I knew it, the construction process was well underway, and I was beginning to feel overwhelmed with loneliness all over again. I did not know who I was any-more. I needed to hear from the Lord.

What I did not realize then (but know now) is that God was recalibrating my life. He was using this season in my life to deposit in me everything I would need to move forward into the new season ahead—a season in which I would step into my dreams, and His dream for me, as a mom, a writer, an author, a speaker. He was using all this to form the message He would have me deliver. In fact, the book you hold in your hand right now is indeed fruit of that very difficult season. God is so good that way.

Here are three keys to help you move forward beyond that wall of loneliness:

1. Trust that God will work each season for your good (see Romans 8:28).
2. Trust what God says in His Word: "I will never leave you nor forsake you" (Hebrews 13:5 NKJV).
3. Trust that what you are experiencing is part of a season and does not have to become your identity. Your name is not *Lonely*. Sure, you may feel this way at times, but that is not who you are. You are a daughter of the Most High God. He sees you, He cares for you and He has an amazing plan for your life.

Remember that even the very hair on your head is numbered. This is how much your heavenly Father cares for you. He is keeping inventory. Even if you have been so stressed that you are losing track of how much hair you have left, be encouraged—your Father knows.

> "Are not two sparrows sold for a penny? Yet not one of them will fall to the ground outside your Father's care. And even the very hairs of your head are all numbered. So don't be afraid; you are worth more than many sparrows."
>
> Matthew 10:29–31

The first chapter in my first book was called "God Cares for You." I wrote about this Scripture and what it meant for Jesus to compare the disciples to a sparrow. *Why a sparrow?* I wondered. I did some research and discovered that, in biblical times, sparrows were considered by merchants to be almost worthless. So even though they still sold them, it was typically at a deep discount. Sometimes it was a sort of "two for a dollar" kind of thing. In this case it would be more accurate to liken it to "five for a penny." That is how little value people placed on the sparrow. But Jesus was saying to the disciples that God cares for the sparrow, even if people don't, because it is one of His creation.

If God cares for a mere sparrow, Jesus was saying, which people deem worthless, how much more do you think He cares for you, the crown of His creation?

> We are God's masterpiece. He has created us anew in Christ Jesus, so we can do the good things he planned for us long ago.
>
> Ephesians 2:10 NLT

Learning more about this blessed me deeply—and I have not even shared the most amazing part with you yet.

As I was leaving my house one afternoon, after working on that chapter, as I closed the front door behind me, I was surprised by a massive flock of sparrows fluttering from the bushes lining the parameter of my front porch. I was only a foot away, and the best way I can describe them is *swarm-like*. I am talking dozens and dozens and dozens of sparrows. Maybe even a hundred or more had been crammed into the six feet or so of bushes along my front porch. I don't quite know how they all fit in there, but somehow they did.

And their flying pattern was like a swarm of bees. They moved in a synchronized manner, all as one. Like a wave they flowed through the air, flying low up from the bushes, moving in my direction, and then, as though catching a breeze, they swooped away from me and landed in the tree just next to my car. There were no leaves on the tree in that season, and the tiny sparrows filled up every last branch. The tree looked as though it had suddenly blossomed little brown flowers—a hundred or more precious little sparrows that God cares about because He made them. How much more does He care for us, my friend?

I had never seen anything like that before and I have not seen anything like it since. It was miraculous. I sat in my car and cried. I cried because I got it. And I cried because I was overwhelmed by the majesty and love of our great big God. He is so real and so big and so near. God was confirming His message that day of how deeply He cares for us by sending an overwhelming number of sparrows—a hundred times over, it would seem—to seal this on my heart.

My friend, as I am writing these words, I am sitting in a hotel lobby on a final push before my writing deadline. I am fighting the overwhelm as I am tucking in with Jesus, trusting He will continue to pour out the message. But just now I heard a woman passing through the lobby saying, "All I need is Jesus." I looked up to see her looking at the television screen in the lobby, and on it were the words *All I need is Jesus*. Apparently the television, which was muted, was tuned to a Christian program. Had she not walked through at that exact moment and read those words aloud, I would not have known they were there.

So even as I sit here writing and reflecting on how present Jesus is in our day-to-day lives and how much God cares, Jesus is smiling over me and saying, *Krissy, if you only knew just how deep and how wide My love is for you, you would never entertain loneliness again.*

For this reason I kneel before the Father, from whom every family in heaven and on earth derives its name. I pray that out of his glorious riches he may strengthen you with power through his Spirit in your inner being, so that Christ may dwell in your hearts through faith. And I pray that you, being rooted and established in love, may have power, together with all the Lord's holy people, to grasp how wide and long and high and deep is the love of Christ, and to know this love that surpasses knowledge—that you may be filled to the measure of all the fullness of God.

Ephesians 3:14–19

The bottom line is this: All we really need is Jesus. And the beautiful thing is, He has been here all along.

Can you hear the wall of loneliness cracking? It is shattering to the ground, my friend.

Believe What God Says about You

"I will never leave you nor forsake you."

Hebrews 13:5 NKJV

Jesus Says: I am with you always.

Declare It: I'm not alone. I am never outside of my Father's care.

Apply It: Write down the areas in your life in which you feel the most alone. Then take your red pen and write over each one, "Jesus is with me."

Prayer

Father, I pray that I will experience the depths of Your great love for me. Anchor me in Your love right now. Wash fresh hope and assurance over me that You are here with me. When life has been the most difficult, You have never lost sight of me. You are pursuing me with Your love even now.

PART 4

I'm Stuck

Definition of *being stuck*

1. To hold to something firmly, as if by adhesion.
2. To become blocked, wedged or jammed.
3. To be unable to proceed.

Mindsets

1. I'm stuck.
2. But I'm not perfect.
3. If I don't mull over every detail, something will get missed.

Walls

1. Being stuck
2. Perfectionism
3. Overthinking

10

I'm Stuck

I'M STUCK. These two little words played through my mind like a broken record as I stared at the blank Word document on the computer screen before me. *Stuck, stuck, stuck. . . .*

As an author I have found that whatever I am writing about, I face personally. So even though I have experienced victory in the area of being stuck—enough to write a book on—I still face it, often in greater measure than before, as I am writing. Essentially it is warfare over the message. I have a testimony that will bring life and hope to those who read, and the enemy is not happy about that. So he launches an attack on the message in hopes that it will never reach you, my amazing reader.

As you can imagine, as I stared at the words *I'm Stuck* as a section and chapter title, the unwanted manifestation of this topic was upon me. On the other hand, it gave me a great opportunity to put into action everything I have learned and planned to share about in the pages of this book.

I was excited about this book from the moment the Lord put it on my heart to write. *Say Goodbye to What Holds You*

Back—to me it does not get much better than that. I felt I was given a gift with this message, and I was thankful and humbled that the Lord would tap me on the shoulder and say, *Hey, Krissy, here's what I want you to write next.* I was ready and excited to go on this journey with Him, as there was still plenty in my own life I was saying goodbye to—old mindsets, past hurts and more. I had seen so many walls shatter to the ground that I felt like a gazelle ready to leap forward full of joy.

But as I stared at those words on the page, *I'm stuck*, I realized that, with no other words to be found, I was also actually, really and truly *stuck!* Though I can almost laugh about the irony of it now, I assure you, there was nothing funny about it at the time.

Now I recognize the reason I was stuck. In addition to the reality of spiritual warfare over the message, it was also because of the season I was in. Everything had compounded, and I was still overwhelmed with everything I had on my plate at the time. I was stretched too thin, and had dealt out my yes to so many others that you could have played a game of checkers with it (or cards; pick one)!

The point is, I was living my message, friend. And truth be told, it was not fun. But as I mentioned earlier, it gave me an opportunity to test the message and apply all the amazing tools and principles God has given me along the way. The outcome is beautiful. Part of the outcome is this finished book. But even more, the outcome is the testimony of Jesus in my life—that He will do what He says He will do. He is our help in times of trouble. He is the Friend who sticks closer than a brother. Our counselor. The Lover of our souls.

For me to move forward looked like what I shared in chapters 7 and 8 about overwhelm and being stretched too thin and needing to remove and restructure some things on my plate so

I could give my book the focus it deserved. I had a part to play, and it started as I sat, prayed and listened to the direction the Lord was giving me.

Friend, there is always a way forward when you feel stuck. Be encouraged; you will find yours, too. For me, in the case of my writing block, I needed to lighten my load and continue listening as Jesus gave me each new step on the journey to becoming unstuck. He came through, and as you can see, I was victorious!

The bottom line: When you feel stuck, wait on the Lord. Don't give up or run the other way. Wait on Him to give you the direction you need so you can—what? You guessed it—keep moving forward. See, you know me well enough by now to guess what I am about to say. Our goal in saying goodbye to what holds us back is to move forward, not allowing any mindset or wall to block us. We will watch these walls shatter to the ground as we believe what God says about us.

In my first book, *Created for the Impossible*, I talk about how God thinks you can do anything. You can be all He has called you to be. He knows it. Why?

> If the Spirit of him who raised Jesus from the dead is living in you, he who raised Christ from the dead will also give life to your mortal bodies because of his Spirit who lives in you.
>
> Romans 8:11

This is why you are created for the impossible. This is why you can slay the giant of fear and say goodbye to what holds you back—because you have resurrection life and power living inside of you! Think about that for a moment. No matter how stuck you may feel, my friend, it is an illusion created to hold you back and hinder you from moving forward in your life.

But not anymore!

The Wall: Being Stuck

The dictionary defines *being stuck* as "holding to something firmly as if by adhesion; becoming blocked, wedged or jammed; being unable to proceed." We can get stuck in what we have always known—for example, firmly held belief systems about ourselves, about life, about the world around us, and about the nature of God.

Feeling stuck can be circumstantial, but we can also feel stuck in general, unable to move forward in life. It is easy for us to feel a bit lost and say things like "I want to, but I can't" or "It's too much" or "I feel like I've lost my way." Sometimes the feeling of being stuck can paralyze us. From our current vantage point, we assess our lives, take inventory of our accomplishments (or lack thereof), and wonder, *How did I end up here?* and, more importantly, *How do I move forward?*

We can become stuck in the following ways:

- Emotionally
- Mentally
- Physically

While I did not write the first four parts of this book to be a progression of events, they certainly can be. We feel as if we are not enough, which scares us and makes us feel overwhelmed, and then stuck, unable to move forward. Our inner dialogue sounds a lot like this:

- This is impossible.
- I'm totally stuck.
- I can't move forward.
- I don't see any other way.

The Trap

The trap is set when we believe the lie that there is no way forward. We think everything hinges on us, on what we can or cannot do, and we stall out. The enemy overcomplicates our way out, causing us to believe that one does not exist or that it is too difficult to get to the other side.

We can all get stuck, friend. Look at the Bible characters we have discussed so far in this book: the woman at the well, Peter, Moses, David, Esther, Jonah, Elijah and the woman washing Jesus' feet with her tears. Each had a mindset that was challenged by what God actually said about them.

The Wall Shatters

The wall shatters when we realize that, through Christ, there is always a way forward. It is not complicated. In fact, it is very straightforward. Jesus makes a way when there is no way.

It is important that you tune your heart not to what you see or don't see around you, but to what God is saying. Then you can align your life with His guidance. Where is He leading you? What is He saying to you? This is where you remain in that "peace pace," remember?—that perfect pace of peace as you follow God's leading as over against what makes the most sense to your mind. The Bible says, "You will keep in perfect peace all who trust in you, all whose thoughts are fixed on you!" (Isaiah 26:3 NLT).

Often our lives will lead us to the shoreline of the impossible. When we arrive, we look around and go, *What was God thinking, leading me here? This looks like the end of the road.*

That was certainly the case with the Hebrew people as Moses led them out of Egypt right up to the shore of the Red Sea. Moses had promised to lead them out of captivity to the

Promised Land. And here they were at what looked to be a dead end. When Pharaoh's armies appeared behind them, horsemen and chariots and all, to capture them, they were trapped! Can you imagine the despair they must have felt? The confusion? The frustration? The fear?

Yet Moses had led them by the route God told him to take.

The interesting thing is, Moses had lived in the desert for forty years so he knew the route to safety, yet he allowed God to take him another way, a circuitous route that would make Pharaoh think they were lost (see Exodus 14:1–3). The outcome was that God confronted the mindset of the people, at the shore of the Red Sea, with the wonder of His unexplainable power.

> Then the LORD said to Moses, "Why are you crying out to me? Tell the Israelites to move on. Raise your staff and stretch out your hand over the sea to divide the water so that the Israelites can go through the sea on dry ground. I will harden the hearts of the Egyptians so that they will go in after them. And I will gain glory through Pharaoh and all his army, through his chariots and his horsemen. The Egyptians will know that I am the LORD when I gain glory through Pharaoh, his chariots and his horsemen."
>
> . . . Then Moses stretched out his hand over the sea, and all that night the LORD drove the sea back with a strong east wind and turned it into dry land. The waters were divided, and the Israelites went through the sea on dry ground, with a wall of water on their right and on their left.
>
> Exodus 14:15–18, 21–22

All glory went to God as Moses lifted his staff and the waters split right down the middle, creating a pathway for the people to move forward on dry land.

Friend, if you are at a place where you can see no way forward, trust that you are serving a God who makes pathways through ocean beds for us to walk through. Nothing is impossible with God. Be at peace and simply trust that He will lead you. You are not stuck; you are waiting on God to reveal His next steps for you.

The wall shatters as you resolve in your heart, *I will follow God's leading no matter what.* When you feel stuck, simply trust that He has the best for you. Remember who God says you are: a champion, more than a conqueror, His daughter, His treasure. He is always working in you and for you to move you forward.

> I am certain that God, who began the good work within you, will continue his work until it is finally finished on the day when Christ Jesus returns.
>
> Philippians 1:6 NLT

Moving Forward

I love working with women who feel stuck, because I can so relate to this feeling.

I made a decision several years ago that I would move forward regardless of how I felt. I would test this thing out. I would push it to its limit until the doors stopped opening and God said, *You've reached your limit, Krissy. No further.* But that has not happened yet. So I continue forward. Not because I think I have all the answers or know some secret that the rest of the world is missing. No, I move forward full of faith simply because I want to see what happens if I take God at His word when He says, *Krissy, I think you can do anything.*

Ultimately it boils down to this: How much do we really believe what God says about us? When He says, "You can" (see, for example, John 14:12 and Philippians 4:13), do you believe Him? Or what about when He says, "Actually, I can," meaning He, God (see Philippians 4:13 and 1 John 4:4), do you trust Him?

Recently, as I was planning to sit down and write, I was overwhelmed with how much I still had left to do. I had awakened really early that Monday morning, way before my kiddos, so I could cozy up on the couch with a cup of coffee and pray. I knew I needed to spend time with the Lord in order to accomplish the task before me. I reached into the cupboard for a coffee mug and had one of those surreal moments that happened so fast I was almost breathless.

I grabbed the handle of one of my favorite inspirational coffee mugs whose message written on the front always encourages me This time God used the words on the mug to speak to me in a brand-new way.

The mug reads *Actually, I Can.* I love this mug. When I read it, I think, *Yes, I can do this.* Whatever it is I am facing, I am reminded—I can do it. It is a wonderfully inspiring message.

But this morning the words were different. As I peered at the mug through the dim lighting of the early morning hour, God spoke to me from the dark gray words painted on the light-colored porcelain, before I could even take it down from the cupboard. I read the words and heard His voice at the same time: *Actually, I Can.* Meaning Him. *He* can.

It is difficult to express just how real and profound this moment was, especially because it happened so fast and was so unexpected. As I placed the mug beneath my single-serve coffee spout and turned it on, I listened as the Father spoke to me yet again: *Don't you see, Krissy? I can.* Then the Holy Spirit said these words: *Through Him.* I was reminded of Philippians 4:13: "I can do everything through Christ, who gives me strength" (NLT). And I heard Holy Spirit's emphasis yet again: *Through Him.*

My coffee had not even finished brewing and I was already crying. I dropped to my knees right there on the kitchen floor and laugh-cried. You know one of those "God is blowing me away" laughs, yet you are so blessed by what has just occurred (and maybe still a bit groggy, if it's early in the morning) that you are also crying? A laugh-cry. That was me at 5:00 a.m. that Monday as I was ambushed pre–coffee by the love of God.

It was powerful to me, my friend. God was reminding me that He is the One who will do this impossible thing. *Through Him.*

Jesus is our pathway forward no matter how stuck we may feel. *Through Him.* He always has been; He always will be. He said, "I am the way, the truth, and the life. No one comes to the Father except *through Me*" (John 14:6 NKJV, emphasis added). So "I can do all this through him who gives me strength" (Philippians 4:13).

Often when we feel stuck, we are in need of a new perspective. This is when it is important to take a step back and press *pause*, similar to that emergency response scenario I shared in chapter 7 when you are feeling overwhelmed: *Stop, breathe and pray.* Likewise, when you are feeling stuck, let's establish an internal protocol: *Pause, process and pray.*

When you are stuck, you will continue to spin your tires if you don't take a step back to pause, process and pray. All three of these are important. When we pause, we can process: What is making me stuck? What mindsets am I holding onto that are preventing me from moving forward? And as we pray, Jesus confronts those mindsets with His voice of truth. He speaks life and hope into our belief systems, stretching our faith and empowering us to move forward out of those old beliefs about ourselves.

Our only role in this process? To move forward in faith, believing what He is saying over the mindsets we have held for so long. We are to be transformed by the renewing of our minds.

Do not conform to the pattern of this world, but be transformed by the renewing of your mind. Then you will be able to test and approve what God's will is—his good, pleasing and perfect will.

Romans 12:2

God's Word says that we are being ever molded into the image of Christ, and that God has given us the mind of Christ.

God knew his people in advance, and he chose them to become like his Son.

Romans 8:29 NLT

For who has known the mind *and* purposes of the Lord, so as to instruct Him? But we have the mind of Christ [to be guided by His thoughts and purposes].

1 Corinthians 2:16 AMP

Say goodbye to being stuck, my friend. We are moving forward through Him who strengthens us, because He can.

Believe What God Says about You

I can do all everything through Christ, who gives me strength.

Philippians 4:13 NLT

Jesus Says: Actually, I can.

Declare It: Through Him. That is how I move forward. Through Jesus.

Apply It: Pause, process and pray. In what areas do you feel stuck? What mindsets are you holding onto? Write them down, circle them with your red pen, and let's agree together that you are moving forward and saying goodbye to what keeps you stuck. Through Him.

Prayer

Father, give me fresh perspective today. Remind me that I can do all things through You. You are my pathway forward. Bring me hope for the journey ahead as this wall of being stuck shatters to the ground.

11

But I'm Not Perfect

I FELT AS IF I WAS LIVING OUT one those scenes in a movie where the viewer is very aware of what the main character needs to do to avoid the crash and burn, but the character has to walk through the storm and fall on her face before she has the same perspective.

I knew I was holding on too tightly, trying to be the best mom, the best wife, the best writer and speaker and friend and person. The list goes on and on. The sensation of holding on so tightly and trying so hard typically leads to the proverbial break we all expect in the movie scene. It is the climactic moment, right?—when the first half of the plot line collides with the second half, when the problem inevitably meets the solution.

But in life we are not always sure if we will find a solution or not. The script has not been written for us. The plotline is unknown.

"I can't do this anymore!" were the last words I remember saying before my head hit my hands and—you guessed it—tears spilled from my eyes.

You know me well enough by now to know that my reaction to overwhelm is tears. It is not that I spend my life in a puddle of tears, but I choose to give you glimpses into these windows of my life journey. By sharing these raw and vulnerable instances with you, my reader, I hope that if I am direct in discussing my breaking points, you will feel comfortable doing the same. It is an important step in the healing process—being real about how we feel, opening up to those we trust in our lives, facing it so we can "cast our cares on the Lord," and then moving forward.

Now the sound of my own sobs echoed through the room. I was exhausted. I had been working nonstop day in and day out toward a certain goal and was just plain done.

What I did not realize at the time was how hard I was trying to be perfect every step of the way. My work needed to be perfect. My response to people needed to be perfect. In order to be successful, nothing in my life should suffer—not my parenting, not my "wife-ing" (yes, I like to make up words!), and certainly not my work. The only thing I would allow to suffer was me. I am not exactly sure how I was able to justify this. Nevertheless, as it goes with perfectionism, I hit the proverbial wall and shut down completely.

Why? Because perfectionism is an unattainable goal that we as Jesus followers are not meant to pursue. The only perfect One is Christ, and our pursuit of Him has to be greater than our pursuit of what is unattainable—our own perfection.

The verse "Be perfect, therefore, as your heavenly Father is perfect" (Matthew 5:48) does not speak to our ability to attain perfection in and of ourselves. This single verse in the context of Jesus' teaching on loving others, concluding His famous Sermon on the Mount, refers to the perfection that will come when we enter glory for eternity. Our aim on the earth is to grow daily in learning to love others as God does.

But here I was in my mid-thirties, struggling as if I were learning this concept for the first time. The concept: My work did not have to be perfect, just my best. But I could not reconcile this with Colossians 3:23: "Whatever you do, work at it with all your heart, as working for the Lord, not for human masters." If I worked at something with all my heart, as unto the Lord, didn't that mean the end product had to be perfect?

No. Nowhere does the Bible say that the only way our effort is successful is by a perfect outcome. That verse in Colossians is speaking of the posture of our hearts, doing everything for the Lord. It is the principle of stewardship, of giving.

I needed to learn more about perfectionism and what God really expected so I could break free from the mindset of "But it's not perfect" and "I'm not perfect" and move forward.

The Wall: Perfectionism

The dictionary defines *perfectionism* as "a disposition to regard anything short of perfection as unacceptable." Perfectionism is a wall that keeps us on the hamster wheel. In our efforts to become perfect, if we are not careful, we will inevitably burn out and fall off the wheel altogether.

The enemy uses perfectionism to ensure that we always feel like a failure. Think about it. Since perfection is unattainable, if that is our aim, we will always have a sense of failure.

Our inner dialogue sounds a lot like this:

- I like everything to be a certain way.
- I try so hard.
- It's not finished unless it's perfect.

Think about our inner gauge. How can we as fallible human beings even gauge perfection? We cannot. So even if we deem a particular outcome as perfect, it is still flawed. Right? Why? Because we have the wrong idea about what "perfect" even is.

I said a minute ago that the only perfect One is Christ. We are not perfect and flawless, not until we are in glory. So we need to let go of the drive toward perfectionism in our day-to-day lives. We must embrace the mess and growth in the journey of learning. We must embrace that the road to maturity and growing in Christ is perfectly messy for us humans.

But the illusion of perfectionism becomes a real wall we face because, as I said, it is unattainable.

The feeling of trying so hard to do perfectly and to be perfect is similar to being stretched too thin (which we discussed in chapter 8). As a woman, you try to be everything for everyone. If you are in the workforce, you hope to excel. If you are married, you aim to be the best wife. If you have kids, you try to be the best mom. The more hats you wear, the more you have to juggle. Eventually all the pressure you put on yourself to be the very best at everything comes tumbling to the ground. Why? Because you are a human being.

Not the answer you were looking for, was it? I promise you, I am smiling right now, but it is just that simple. You are a human being. You will drop the ball from time to time. And you know something? That is okay. (I have to tell myself this regularly, if not every day!)

The Trap

The trap is set when we believe perfection means the same as giving it our best. But there is a difference between perfectionism and the call to us as Jesus followers toward excellence, faithfulness, commitment.

We often misunderstand Jesus' call and commissioning with how we execute. We give Him our yes and take steps forward in faith like a child . . . but along the way, as we learn, we think, *Okay, now I've got this. Now I know what to do.* And we compete with ourselves, wanting to perfect this model, when Jesus is over there saying simply, *Come, follow Me.*

Jesus does not expect your execution to be perfect; He simply asks for your heart to be willing. His command is this:

> "If anyone would come after me, let him deny himself and take up his cross and follow me. For whoever would save his life will lose it, but whoever loses his life for my sake will find it."
>
> Matthew 16:24–25 ESV

As I have wrestled with perfectionism, I have had to make very conscious decisions to let go of my need for what I consider perfect and embrace the reality of the Kingdom—which is my obedience. This is very freeing. It enables me to continue moving forward in the call on my life to abandon perfectionism and thrive in who God created me to be—flaws, limits, quirks and all.

I have discovered that if we do not let go, burnout is inevitable. You might even be at that place right now in your walk. I want to encourage you—you are not alone. And you are not too far gone, either. Begin to make a conscious choice starting right now: *I don't want to live like this anymore.* And ask Jesus to help you. Listen: "The kingdom of God is not a matter of eating and drinking, but of righteousness, peace and joy in the Holy Spirit" (Romans 14:17)

There is fresh hope, peace and joy for you today, my friend. Jesus can do in one second what you can search a lifetime for and never attain in your own effort.

We learn from the story of Mary and Martha the difficult time Martha had in letting go of her own default to prepare and perfect. When Jesus was visiting her home, she went right into prep mode. After all, this was Jesus, different from anyone else—although Martha may not have been fully aware at the time as to how or why He was different.

Her sister, Mary, had fresh insight we can all glean from. She sat at Jesus' feet listening, worshiping. Mary had no inclination toward perfection. She was sitting at the lowest place, the floor, at His feet, and every fiber of her being told her this was the only place to be.

> But Martha was distracted by all the preparations that had to be made. She came to him and asked, "Lord, don't you care that my sister has left me to do the work by myself? Tell her to help me!"
>
> "Martha, Martha," the Lord answered, "you are worried and upset about many things, but few things are needed—or indeed only one. Mary has chosen what is better, and it will not be taken away from her."
>
> Luke 10:40–42

It is not that Martha could have done anything different in the moment. Serving the Lord in her own home may have been a new experience for her, even if she did not fully know *who* was in her midst. But we do, and we can glean from this story the most important posture to take when it comes to Christ: total submission. Allow Him to communicate the next steps we take.

It would have been interesting to see what would have occurred if Martha had asked Jesus what He preferred she do. Perhaps He would have said, "Martha, I know you find great joy in the preparations, so please, go and prepare—that sounds amazing." Or He might have invited her to sit with Him in the living room or at the table because He was not really there for food anyway.

The point is not Martha getting it right or wrong in this scenario; the point is, did she learn? Would she do it differently next time? Did she realize that perfect hosting or a perfect meal wasn't what Jesus was after, but her heart? Jesus had not come to their home to be served, but to serve. This was unheard of in this time, because they were women.

I am thankful for this story so I can have a stronger understanding that when Jesus walks into the room, He wants to spend time with me. May I always fall at His feet and listen and worship Him! If perfectionism or performance is what I am aiming for, I can lay it at His feet.

Friends, this is the invitation from Christ: He desires time with us. Concepts of success, high quality and excellence don't look like "perfection" in the Kingdom; they simply look like faithfulness. Have we fulfilled our part and did we do it unto the Lord? When we receive this freedom from Jesus, knowing we are off the hook for the perfect outcome, we move from surviving to thriving.

The Wall Shatters

The wall shatters right now as you let go and sit at Jesus' feet. He is the perfect One, so you don't need to be. Friend, may we repent for hanging on so tightly to what we try to do in our own strength, and surrender all over again to Jesus. He is the way forward. He always has been, He always will be. It really is that simple.

As I mentioned earlier, perfectionism can make us feel as though we are on a hamster wheel, not making any progress. Today you can decide to get off the wheel and start afresh, right here, right now.

You don't have to be perfect.

It doesn't have to be perfect.

You simply continue to show up in obedience with a heart to serve, loving Jesus and loving others. Watch as the wall of "But I'm not perfect" comes crashing to the ground. Today is your day of freedom. Be revived in Christ so you can thrive in who God created you to be. Wild and free—no need for perfect here. Hurray!

The answer to perfectionism is letting go of our need for perfection, whether within ourselves or toward what we are putting our hands to. There is a root of fear in perfectionism. "If I don't make it perfect, it could fail" or "This might not be good enough if I don't perfect it." Can you hear the issue in these words? Perfectionism becomes more about your ability to accomplish something than about Christ's ability to accomplish it through you.

It is important for us to acknowledge our own limits and allow the Lord to use us right where we are, limits and all. Limits are actually a good thing. As my dad always says, limits are guideposts reminding us along the way of our need for Jesus. That is why the apostle Paul could boast in his own weakness, or limits, because it was there that God's power is perfected (see 2 Corinthians 12:9).

Moving Forward

I spent many years trying never to drop the ball that when I did, I was so hard on myself. But I have learned that avoiding imperfection is not possible; what is more important is my mindset. My attitude. Being okay with my imperfections, seeing them as another opportunity for God's power to be perfected in me and for Christ to work in me and through me.

So . . . course-correct as needed. Don't worry so much about the storm that you do not take off and soar; simply find another way, or make the necessary adjustments so you can fly right through if you need to. The key is not perfection; it is simply that you move forward.

Course-correcting is essential in moving forward when we feel stuck. Often we will stall out waiting for the storm to pass when God is motioning us forward regardless. Life is filled with storms; we cannot allow ourselves to become stuck on the ground, unwilling to fly through a storm, if we see Jesus motioning us forward.

That is what occurred with Peter in the story we looked at in chapter 5. In the middle of the storm that was buffeting the boat, the disciples saw Jesus standing out on the water. Peter stepped out of the boat and walked toward Jesus in obedience to His call. We see how powerful this was and how Peter walked atop the impossible empowered by Jesus, safe because Jesus was calling him to move forward.

I spoke with a family friend who is a retired airline pilot. When asked about flying through storms, he said, "The first step is to avoid the storm altogether." Before takeoff, he said, they gather all the information they can about the weather conditions, and if the data suggest a storm, they delay the flight to avoid it. I asked him about when they are already in the air and learn there is a storm ahead. This is when a course correction is warranted, he said. They may change course thirty degrees or so to avoid the storm. When there is no choice but to fly through the storm, certain alterations are needed, such as alerting the passengers and clearing the aisleways.

So what is essential for us? Seeing Jesus motioning us forward.

My friend, if you have gotten off track, simply course-correct today. We cannot achieve perfection; what we need is Jesus. In everything and for everything, He is our source of strength. And as we draw on Him, an overwhelming peace follows that allows us to abandon the need for perfection. So we face that wall and watch it tumble to the ground.

When you feel yourself leaning toward perfectionism, take a deep breath and remind yourself, it doesn't need to be perfect. Ask yourself, *Am I giving it my best?* If the answer is yes, you are on the right track. Peace will surround you as you finish what you started, leaving the outcome to the Father.

Believe What God Says about You

You did not receive the spirit of bondage again to fear, but you received the Spirit of adoption by whom we cry out, "Abba, Father."

Romans 8:15 NKJV

Jesus Says: I am the perfect One; you can lean on Me.

Declare It: I don't need to be perfect—Jesus is. It doesn't need to be perfect—Jesus is. I am letting go today, shattering the wall and walking into freedom, thriving in who God created me to be.

Apply It: Write down the areas in which you experience perfectionism. Take your red pen and write the words *Jesus is perfect* over the top of each of those areas.

Prayer

Father, move me from perfectionism to perfect peace in You. I surrender my need to be perfect and make things perfect, allowing You to take over and have Your way in my life. Help me thrive in who You created me to be by shattering this wall and stepping into freedom with Jesus. Amen.

12

If I Don't Mull over Every Detail, Something Will Get Missed

JUST FOR FUN, let's pretend we are in a group setting right now. By a show of hands, would say you are prone to overthinking? Come on now, don't be shy.

I just paused writing so I could raise both my hands and my two legs, too, ensuring that, if you could see me, you would rest assured that I have very much struggled with overthinking. I still can if I am not careful. So much so that as I typed out the chapter title, I thought to myself, *Oh my, I don't know if I can write this chapter. There's so much to say about overthinking. Where would I even start?* [Laughter.] I kid you not, my friend. True story.

But is this not the case with us women? We overthink—we just do. We like to weigh all the options and assess every last detail. We ponder, we pray, we seek advice, we solicit wise counsel, we Google, and then we start the whole process over again and repeat as necessary.

Say this after me: *Overcomplicating leads to overthinking, and overthinking leads to overcomplicating.* What more can I say? The wall of overthinking is very real and can make us feel stuck.

As you know by now, friend, my entire life's journey has been about breaking down walls one by one—pushing through with wild abandon as God declares over me, *Krissy, I think you can do anything.* (I told you that powerful story in chapter 1.) I have listened to each wall shatter to the ground as I move forward with Jesus. The only way I have been able to do this is through the grace of God in my life, cooperating with Him as He guides me. It has not always been easy, and I have hit many bumps, detours and pitfalls along the way.

But as I write and reflect on where I was and where I am now, and all the mindsets I have partnered with over the years, I am overwhelmed at God's goodness to lead me out of them. I think about His goodness as I simply sit in His presence and listen. *What are You saying, Jesus? Wash my mind with Your Word. Speak truth into the lies. Shatter every wall.*

Overthinking was the most recent mindset to overcome, and one of the most difficult. That mindset says, *If I don't mull over every detail, something will get missed.* As a result, my life was riddled with anxiety, stress and overwhelm. Sleepless nights became my norm. I carried a false sense of responsibility for the success of our family—responsibility I did not need to carry. I thought, *If I can't produce what's expected of me, everything will collapse. We will lose everything.* I became fixated on the pressure, fearing that I did not have enough time to accomplish all that was on my plate. This resulted in wasting the time I *did* have on worry. I was exhausted. I needed to be free from overthinking. But how?

The nature of overthinking says that everything will unravel if you lose sight of even one detail. *Don't take your eye off the prize. Keep your eye on the ball. It's up to you. It all hinges on you.* It is exhausting, isn't it?

As we take a step back, it is easier to recognize how anti–Kingdom this is. Let's look at the contrasts:

- Jesus says, "Surrender. Cast all your cares on Me. Deny yourself. Die daily."
- Overthinking says, "I'm losing my grip. I need to hang on more tightly. I need to be stronger."

The key to shattering this wall is when we finally, totally and utterly let go.

Yikes! Let go? But we have worked so hard to maintain our grip, right?

Friend, it is time to let go.

Letting go is when the presence of God came crashing in for me, my friend. The answer is time in His presence. There is no other way or workaround. Why? Because in His presence our minds are renewed and our lives experience transformation.

You see, the Bible clearly states that while we live in this world, we are not to be like this world. The world's way of solving problems is to focus on what is wrong and everything we need to do to make it right. The Kingdom way of solving problems is to let go of everything and cast all our cares onto Jesus so He can work them out for our good and His glory. "Give all your worries and cares to God, for he cares about you" (1 Peter 5:7 NLT).

Romans reminds us of the Kingdom approach to problem solving and letting go of unhealthy mindsets:

Here's what I want you to do, God helping you: Take your everyday, ordinary life—your sleeping, eating, going-to-work, and walking-around life—and place it before God as an offering. Embracing what God does for you is the best thing you can do for him. Don't become so well-adjusted to your culture that you fit into it without even thinking. Instead, fix your attention on God. You'll be changed from the inside out. Readily recognize what he wants from you, and quickly respond to it. Unlike the culture around you, always dragging you down to its level of immaturity, God brings the best out of you, develops well-formed maturity in you.

Romans 12:1–2 MSG

The Wall: Overthinking

The dictionary defines *overthinking* as "thinking too much about something; putting too much time into analyzing something in a way that is more harmful than helpful."

Overthinking is like over-strategizing. We often do this under the guise of being proactive since, as women and especially as mothers, we can often see a few steps ahead and will try to control the outcome if we can.

Our inner dialogue sounds a lot like this:

- I can't seem to turn off my brain.
- I wish I could change what I did in the past.
- I'm so worried about everything.
- I feel like everything hinges on my ability to be proactive.

Have you ever heard the phrase *analysis paralysis*? The more you think, the worse you feel. We can become stuck in our analysis and never move forward into positive change.

It is easy to confuse overthinking with problem solving and positive self-evaluation for the purposes of learning and growing. But there is a big difference. Problem solving focuses on the solution; overthinking focuses mainly on the problem. A person who is overthinking often fixates on the problem and cannot move into solution mode. This can create high levels of anxiety, worry, overwhelm and fear, giving us the overall feeling of being stuck. It is a wall that needs to shatter to the ground.

The difference between overthinking and healthy self-evaluation for the purpose of being teachable is also very distinct. When I keep myself in a place of continual learning, I am focused on areas in which I can grow and make positive change through a fresh perspective and healthier mindset. There is purpose in it. Overthinking, on the other hand, whether on my behavior, my responses or my mistakes, focuses on how bad I feel, and I begin to fixate on things I have little to no control over. It lacks purpose and does not help me grow.

Overthinking triggers a whole slew of anxiety, fear, worry, overwhelm—all the segments of this book, really. The wall it creates makes us feel stuck—paralyzed, even. We cannot move forward because we cannot face all the worrisome problems that could arise. We become fixated on the past, anxious about the future, or both.

How do we move forward? How do we get out on the other side of this wall? Better yet, how can we watch the wall of overthinking shatter to the ground? First let's take a look at the trap that is set.

The Trap

The trap is set when we believe overthinking is being proactive. Isn't that just like the enemy, to make a negative sound like a positive? But this is exactly what he does—and it is the essence of deception. It seems reasonable and has some element of truth to it.

Just discussing this reminds me of the dialogue Moses had with God, which we discussed in chapter 3. He debated all the reasons he was not the best option to communicate to Pharaoh and lead the Israelites out of Egypt. Moses' arguments seemed reasonable, at least to him, but God had a plan for choosing Moses, and it was not about his strength in communicating. Moses was indeed overthinking. He was focused only on the problem—his poor communication skills—instead of the solution: "Oh, I see, God! Since I'm weak in this area into which You are calling me, I can assume You will speak through me."

When it comes to who God says you are or how He is calling you, there is no need for overthinking. Yet we often do.

Gideon spent time overthinking when the Lord appeared to him. Gideon had been going about his day-to-day activity of threshing wheat in a winepress—hiding it from their oppressors, the Midianites—when the Lord appeared to him and said, "The Lord is with you, mighty warrior." Mighty warrior? Gideon had never fought a battle in his life. He was just as troubled over the danger facing his people as the next guy. It had never crossed his mind that God would see him as part of the solution. But God had other plans.

> "Pardon me, my lord," Gideon replied, "but if the Lord is with us, why has all this happened to us? Where are all his wonders that our ancestors told us about when they said, 'Did not the Lord bring us up out of Egypt?' But now the Lord has abandoned us and given us into the hand of Midian."
>
> The Lord turned to him and said, "Go in the strength you have and save Israel out of Midian's hand. Am I not sending you?"
>
> "Pardon me, my lord," Gideon replied, "but how can I save Israel? My clan is the weakest in Manasseh, and I am the least in my family."

The Lord answered, "I will be with you, and you will strike down all the Midianites, leaving none alive."

Gideon replied, "If now I have found favor in your eyes, give me a sign that it is really you talking to me. Please do not go away until I come back and bring my offering and set it before you."

And the Lord said, "I will wait until you return."

Judges 6:13–18

Gideon did come back with an offering, as he promised. But he went on to mull over this new identity God was speaking over him, and for a few days he tested the call. I mentioned in chapter 9 the fleece that Gideon asked God to make first wet, then dry, to confirm His leading. God, in His mercy, was patient, and Gideon ultimately let go of his need to figure it all out and moved forward as the mighty warrior God said he was. The resulting military victory over the Midianites was won in a way that only God could have done. (Read the story in Judges 7.)

We have to remember that God knows the end from the beginning. He is Alpha and Omega, the beginning and the end. So when He looks at you, He sees who you are becoming. This may shock you, because who you are becoming is always part of the solution to the crisis around you. But you are a soldier in the Lord's army. You have a divine purpose on this earth to "go into all the world and preach the gospel to all creation" (Mark 16:15).

The big picture is this: The world is broken. The solution is this: "You will receive power when the Holy Spirit comes on you; and you will be my witnesses" (Acts 1:8). What He says about you and His plans for you are more amazing than you can even fathom, my friend. Could it be that you, like Esther, were put on this earth, in your city, in your community, for such a time as this?

The Wall Shatters

The wall shatters when we focus on Kingdom solutions over present problems. Let's never forget what the Word teaches us about being teachable. We are clay in the hands of our Potter. "We are the clay, and you are the potter. We all are formed by your hand" (Isaiah 64:8 NLT). We must not resist the process of being molded and shaped.

Trust that God has a plan and that you do not have to have everything figured out. And embrace that you are a work in progress. Don't try to be five million steps ahead as you fixate on avoiding problems. Be as proactive as you can, yes. But then do what is right and leave the outcome to the Lord. What is right? Surrender. Obedience. Faithfulness. Do your best and leave the rest to God as you sit back and rest, knowing you will hit bumps along the way—and that is perfectly normal.

My dad always reminds me that my journey is like a game of bumper bowling. The bumpers are in place to nudge me gently back on track as I go. I try to remain faithful, doing my best to stay on track, but I have to be okay with the process and know that the bumpers are there for a reason. "Every child of God overcomes the world, for our faith is the victorious power that triumphs over the world" (1 John 5:4 TPT).

Moving Forward

There have been many seasons in my life where I was paralyzed by overthinking. I became gripped by concern that there was only one ideal scenario and it was up to me to mull over every detail until I landed on just the right option. I wonder if you can relate?

In middle school I learned that a way to cope was simply to tuck away in my room and never exit so as to not get in anyone's way. I avoided the people and the problems in my life. I remember watching movies in which the fascinating main character would enter people's lives and, while first making a mess of things, end up becoming someone the others could not imagine their lives without. I used to envy this type of person. The one unafraid to ruffle feathers, drop into people's lives and make some waves. I saw these characters as unapologetically themselves.

I deeply desired this for myself but had no idea how to let go of the crippling fear I had that I would only make people's lives more complicated. I was your classic overthinker—ruminating on things I had no control over, worrying incessantly about the unknown journey before me.

Over time this fear became less. One of the saving graces in my life was meeting the man of my dreams when I was still quite young. Donovan and I married just before my twentieth birthday, and now, more than two decades later, he remains as a rock in my life. I tell him all the time that I believe God sent him to me at such a young age to save me from myself. Donovan's name means *warrior*, and he has truly been that in my life, helping me to "keep it simple, Krissy," as he often says, which prevents my overthinking brain from—well, overthinking.

We all need warriors in our lives, friend—those who lift our arms when we are weak and fight for us when we lack the strength to fight for ourselves. This can be a spouse or friend or family member. I encourage you to find a fellow warrior, and to be a warrior in someone else's life as well.

Year after year, season after season of pausing, processing and praying, I have seen God take a hammer to each and every wall, shattering them to the ground so His daughter can run wild and free into her future. Can you guess that I am now crying as I write this?—because God is so good. What a gift it is to be able to let go!

Listen, overthinking can be normal. The act in and of itself is not so much the issue. The issue is if we don't land on letting go and letting Jesus take over. Cast your cares on Christ, my friend. Don't resist the simple solutions Jesus offers just because they do not make sense to you. Trust that God has a plan. As His Word says, His ways are higher than ours:

> "My thoughts are not your thoughts, neither are your ways my ways," declares the LORD. "As the heavens are higher than the earth, so are my ways higher than your ways and my thoughts than your thoughts."
>
> Isaiah 55:8–9

A key to stopping overthinking is keeping it simple. Focus on the solution, not the problem. And our solution as believers may simply be Jesus. We can trust that God has the plan and we can rest in Him.

Here is one of my favorite verses: "Trust in the LORD with all your heart, and lean not on your own understanding; in all your ways acknowledge Him, and He shall direct your paths" (Proverbs 3:5–6 NKJV). These verses have been a lifesaver for me as I have overcome analysis paralysis—that is, overthinking. These verses remind me that I am not called to have all the answers or weigh every little detail; I am called to trust the One who does. He says, "I am GOD. At the right time I'll make it happen" (Isaiah 60:22 MSG).

Move forward today, my friend. Let go completely, allowing God to offer His fresh perspective on your life and on every last detail. He has the plan. He loves you and knows you can do anything. He has placed His Spirit inside you to empower you and ensure that you can and will move forward.

So surrender all your worries to Him and feel a fresh wind of refreshing life and hope blowing over you now. Can you hear the wall of overthinking shatter to the ground?

Believe What God Says about You

Trust in the LORD with all your heart, and lean not on your own understanding; in all your ways acknowledge Him, and He shall direct your paths.

Proverbs 3:5–6 NKJV

Jesus Says: Simply trust Me and let go.

Declare It: I will trust the Lord and not my own understanding. I cast my cares on You, Jesus.

Apply It: Write down the areas in which you have a tendency to overthink. Where have you had a difficult time letting go? Take out your red pen and write the name *Jesus* on top of each bullet point.

Prayer
Father, help me walk in simple obedience to You and with deeper trust in You. I am who You say I am. I don't need to overthink or have all the answers. I trust in You. Thank You. In Jesus' name. Amen.

PART 5

I'm Free!

Definition of *free*

1. Not bound, confined or detained by force.
2. Not confined to a particular position or place.
3. To relieve or rid of what restrains, confines, restricts or embarrasses.

Mindsets

1. I'm free!
2. I'm moving forward.
3. I'm saying hello to all that God has for me.

13

I'm Free!

JESUS LOVES YOU. I found this timely reminder in the most obscure place, beautifully stenciled on the back of a garbage truck, of all things. Had the timing not lined up the way it did, I would never have seen it.

Ironically, it was time, or lack thereof, that had me in a tizzy as I drove down the back road near our subdivision to avoid as much traffic as possible. You see, I was in a hurry. I was in a hurry a lot those days. And I was making my frustrations known to the Lord as I traveled the bumpy side road.

I was tired. As usual I had been juggling a lot—project deadlines, recuperating from the busy holiday season, the kids being out of school, sicknesses, family in town, and more. Now the kids were back in school and I was playing catch-up.

This particular afternoon I was doing my best to make it to the seamstress before she closed. It was one of those days that hinged on everything going according to plan in order for everyone to get where they needed to be and have what they needed to have. I had to pick up my daughter's cheer uniform from the seamstress so I could be back home for an online meeting that I had to cut off as soon as it ended so I could get to my daughter's school before her game. Thus, the hurry and the grumbling.

I was thinking about all the events of the year prior that had created a snowball effect, causing this particular day to be as stressful as it was. I am sure the look on my face reflected my inner war. Thankfully no one was around as I grumbled aloud the many "if-then" scenarios that should have or could have played out differently, which would have made these next couple weeks much less stressful. *If this one event hadn't gone that way and if that project had ended sooner and if I had made a different decision with that, then . . .*

You get the idea. I was teetering into overthinking land. Thankfully the Lord intervened with one simple question: *But did you learn the lessons?*

And just like that, all my complaining ceased and I felt the presence of God fill my car. Immediately I repented for all my complaints, because I got it. I heard loud and clear the message inside the question. I have so much to be thankful for. I should not be complaining. I should be welcoming the opportunities in each season to learn and grow. I should be expressing gratitude for all God has done for me and my family.

"I'm so sorry, Lord, forgive me. Yes, I'm learning the lessons. I am now, anyway. Thank You for all Your many blessings over this last year." I took a deep breath, and exhaled. I felt peace.

That was when I saw the garbage truck. Turning the corner, I began to slow down as I noticed this old metal garbage truck up ahead of me. His turn signal was on so I knew he would be turning left. I was still processing the Lord's question when I came to a stop behind the garbage truck. Then I saw them—those timely words that had been stenciled on the back of this old truck: *Jesus Loves You.*

I gulped as the truck made its turn and I continued forward. Scrambling, I managed to snap a picture of the back of the truck. I think I wanted to double check that I really did see what I saw, because it was all very surreal and, as usual, it occurred so fast. Another garbage truck happened to pull out of the empty lot in front of me, and there were no words to be found on the back of that truck. It was just the one.

I continued to process what the Lord was saying. Did I learn the lessons? Well, I was learning them now, that was for sure. Basically all my complaining was—well, garbage. It deserved to be thrown into the trash and taken away in the garbage truck. What is more, Jesus loves me so much He will gladly take my garbage to the dump for me, because that is what He does.

I could still see a glimpse of that amazing "Jesus loves you" garbage truck in my rearview mirror as I drove farther away until I could no longer see it. What a profound moment! I felt I was truly saying goodbye to what was trying to hold me back—all the garbage of old mindsets and the ruins of shattered walls. And then it was gone, and so was I. I was moving forward and I was free.

Friend, regardless of what has gone on in your life, I encourage you, don't go into complaining land. Take the grumbling to the garbage dump where it belongs and say goodbye. Jesus will even drive it there for you!—because He loves you. Focus on this question: Did I learn the lessons?

Our challenges in life create opportunities for us to learn and grow, if we let them. Remember these principles:

> Whatever is true, whatever is noble, whatever is right, whatever is pure, whatever is lovely, whatever is admirable—if anything is excellent or praiseworthy—think about such things. Whatever

you have learned or received or heard from me, or seen in me—put it into practice. And the God of peace will be with you.

Philippians 4:8–9

Keep your mind on all things lovely, and give thanks for everything Jesus has done for you. Focus on learning the lessons as you keep moving forward, farther and farther away from the debris.

Time to Say Goodbye

Friend, it is time to say goodbye to what has been holding you back once and for all. As we have discussed throughout this book, the attack is to keep you from moving forward. So it is vital that you walk away from those remnant pieces of the shattered wall behind you and keep on walking. Really. Fill up that garbage truck, friend, and allow Jesus to drive away with all the wreckage.

Let's review the many mindsets you have overcome:

1. I'll never be good enough.
2. There's something wrong with me.
3. Someone else can do it better.
4. I'm so afraid.
5. But I might fail.
6. I don't want to ruffle any feathers.
7. I'm so overwhelmed.
8. I'm not good at saying no.
9. I'm all alone.
10. I'm stuck.
11. But I'm not perfect.
12. If I don't mull over every detail, something will get missed.

The walls that we have shattered:

1. Shame
2. Insecurity
3. Comparison
4. Fear
5. Fear of failure
6. People pleasing
7. Overwhelm
8. Being stretched too thin
9. Loneliness
10. Being stuck
11. Perfectionism
12. Overthinking

Moving Forward

The enemy would love nothing more than for you to feel regret over your past, in order to hinder you moving forward with the simple tools you have now gleaned. Don't buy into this.

Here is something I remind myself if I am slipping into regret over the past or worry over the future: *I can't change the past. I can't control the future. But I can decide today to do my best.* This helps me keep my Jesus perspective as I continue to move forward in freedom.

> You make known to me the path of life; in your presence there is fullness of joy; at your right hand are pleasures forevermore.
>
> Psalm 16:11 esv

Begin again. Just the other day as I was in prayer, the Holy Spirit spoke very clearly: *Begin again.* Over and over, I heard these words rolling around in my spirit: *Begin again.* I thought about all the times I have felt as if I was starting over yet again. It occurred to me as I pondered these words from the Holy Spirit that there is no shame in beginning again, and again, and again. As I chewed on this truth, I went to the whiteboard in my office. (Well, truth be told, it is nestled right now in my entryway because my house is a mess, and I am trying to reorganize—again!) But I wrote the words *Begin again.*

As I stared at these words, and the mess of boxes and clutter and remnants of holiday décor I was trying to organize while juggling many other tasks and projects, I felt a refreshing breeze brush past my face. I took a deep breath and realized I don't have to fear beginning again if it means I keep trying. Prompted by the Holy Spirit, I then wrote the following on my whiteboard: *It's okay to begin again; the travesty would be if you didn't.*

How often do we fear restarting because we think we should be farther along? This is a mindset we want to avoid, my friend. This can bring us right back into that place of feeling stuck. And we are saying goodbye to being stuck, aren't we? In fact, we have already parted ways. We are free!

Jesus died to give you a fresh start, so that you *could* be free. He wore the chains of this life so you could break free from your prison of worry, fear, shame, sin, insecurity—all of it! Friend, there is nothing you cannot do with Christ. Who does He say you are today? What is He speaking over you? What have you been delivered from? The time for you to declare the goodness of God is now.

Because you are free!

Believe What God Says about You

Christ has set us free to live a free life. So take your stand! Never again let anyone put a harness of slavery on you.

Galatians 5:1 MSG

Jesus Says: I love you. You are free!

Declare It: Jesus loves me. I am free!

Apply It: Write in your journal these three simple words today: *I am free!*

Prayer

Father, thank You for making all things new and leading me into freedom. Let Your joy fill my heart today as I declare these words over myself: I am free. *In Jesus' name. Amen.*

14

I'm Moving Forward

AN ARMY IS ARISING, awakened to the power of God on the inside and ready to move forward full of faith.

There is a reason you have held this book in your hand and heard these walls shatter. God wants you free and wide awake to who you are in Him.

A champion.

A warrior.

A friend of God.

What wouldn't we do for our friends? What wouldn't we do for the One who has awakened our souls and rescued us from the pit?

God has marked you as His beloved daughter. He thinks you can do anything; He knows it. Friend, what you have been dealing with is the battle for your soul. The enemy wants you worn down, feeling "less than"—afraid, overwhelmed, stuck, without hope. But he has not been victorious, has he? "We have this hope as an anchor for the soul" (Hebrews 6:19).

Often after a battle, we wonder, *How will I have the strength to do this again?* My battle-weary friend, know that God is with you, breathing new life in you to keep you moving forward. Jesus is the one who puts us back together so we can begin again, fresh and new. Do you remember what God did for the army that was nothing but a valley of dead, dry bones? Let's take a look at that story and remember the power of God.

His people had been exiled by King Nebuchadnezzar to Babylon. All hope was lost—so much so that they were likened to a valley of dead, dry bones. One of those taken into captivity was Ezekiel, one of God's messengers on the earth. God told him, "They are saying, 'We have become old, dry bones—all hope is gone'" (Ezekiel 37:11 NLT). But He gave Ezekiel a vision.

> The LORD took hold of me, and I was carried away by the Spirit of the LORD to a valley filled with bones. He led me all around among the bones that covered the valley floor. They were scattered everywhere across the ground and were completely dried out. Then he asked me, "Son of man, can these bones become living people again?"
>
> "O Sovereign LORD," I replied, "you alone know the answer to that."
>
> Ezekiel 37:1–3 NLT

Can you relate to the feeling of hope being lost—so lost that it is piled up in a graveyard with the rest of your dreams? Isn't it interesting that in this story, though God was fully aware of the answer, He asked Ezekiel, "Can these dead bones live again?"

Often God will ask us a question in order to make us think. He does this to awaken hope inside us, causing us to partner with Him for what seems impossible and positioning us as part of the unlikely solution.

Ezekiel answered the way I think I would as well: "Only You know the answer to that, Lord." If Ezekiel's hope was lost, what hope was there for everyone else? But God gave instructions:

> Then he said to me, "Speak a prophetic message to these bones and say, 'Dry bones, listen to the word of the LORD! This is what the Sovereign LORD says: Look! I am going to put breath into you and make you live again! I will put flesh and muscles on you and cover you with skin. I will put breath into you, and you will come to life. Then you will know that I am the LORD.'"
>
> verses 4–6 NLT

God was asking Ezekiel to prophesy life to those bones, to what had died, jumpstarting the revival of hope.

Often when we go through challenging seasons, we become weary warriors. I believe God wants to breathe on your dry bones right here, right now. His Spirit is breathing on you and reviving your heart to new life. Where the enemy tried to shut you down and take you out, God is calling you to rise up. He is saying, "Daughter, get up and get moving. Hope is not lost."

When Ezekiel prophesied life to those dry bones, at the Lord's direction,

> there was a rattling noise all across the valley. The bones of each body came together and attached themselves as complete skeletons. Then as I watched, muscles and flesh formed over the bones. Then skin formed to cover their bodies, but they still had no breath in them.
>
> Then he said to me, "Speak a prophetic message to the winds, son of man. Speak a prophetic message and say, 'This is what the Sovereign LORD says: Come, O breath, from the four winds! Breathe into these dead bodies so they may live again.'"

So I spoke the message as he commanded me, and breath came into their bodies. They all came to life and stood up on their feet—a great army.

verses 7–10 NLT

Revival was coming to the people of Israel and they did not even realize it. God was refilling their hearts with hope. It started with one willing participant, Ezekiel. That is all it took.

As you say goodbye to what has held you back, take some time to reflect on all the Lord has done. Get ready for all He is about to do in and through you as you believe what He says about you.

Reflection

1. What primary walls were you dealing with?
2. What mindsets did you overcome?
3. What is God saying to you?
4. How will you move forward?
5. What is your vision?

Write these things down as you move forward.

Let's be a generation of women who run boldly toward freedom, who are not afraid to shine the light and hope of Christ brightly to the world around us. Friend, the world needs Jesus. God is looking for those who will be His voice on the earth today to speak hope to the hopeless. They need a bridge from their hopelessness to the hope that is found in knowing Christ. You are that bridge, and God is making you stronger and breathing new life into you today. Allow Him to wash over you right now.

Moving Forward

As you move forward in freedom, remember to give yourself grace in the process. Life keeps going but new mindsets take time and repetition to stick, and you need to heal and regroup. Spend time with the Lord and with a trusted friend or family member, talking about what God has done in you.

Friend, as I have journeyed this process, it has taken me weeks, sometimes months, to decompress. Don't rush the process. Remember your limits; they are there for a reason. They remind us of our total dependency on Jesus. They draw us closer to Him. And they are meant to protect us, reminding us that we need to slow down and recharge.

Remember, too, the old mindsets that pop up are not what keep us stuck; it is how frequently we buy into them. The more we allow those mindsets to influence our choices and how we see ourselves, the more building blocks are added to the walls that hinder our moving forward.

As you go, when you hear a lie or mindset come up, continue to move forward in obedience to what you know is right. You can ignore the lie, paying it no mind, as you focus on what God is saying to you. Who does He say you are? What has He called you to move forward in?

Here are three things you can do to ensure that positive change truly sticks:

1. Repeat those Jesus declarations over yourself daily.
2. When a negative thought reminiscent of an old mindset pops up, say the name of Jesus and declare who He says you are. Move forward out of obedience to God's call regardless of how you feel.
3. Get into the habit of focusing on solutions and on moving forward.

Here are three things you can do if you find an old mindset creeping in:

1. Don't panic. This does not mean the wall is resurrected; it simply means you used to think that way in the past.
2. Trust the Lord. He is faithful to see to completion the good work He is doing in you.
3. Declare, "I'm moving forward."

Get your hopes way up, my friend. Remember that God sees you as His beautiful, beloved daughter. He thinks you can do anything, including saying goodbye to what has held you back, so you can move forward with Him. Do you believe it?

Believe What God Says about You

"I know the plans I have for you," declares the Lord, "plans to prosper you and not to harm you, plans to give you hope and a future."

Jeremiah 29:11

Jesus Says: You are moving forward.

Declare It: I am moving forward.

Apply It: After completing the reflection questions above, take out your red pen and write these words at the end of your notebook: "I am moving forward and Jesus is helping me."

Prayer

Father, thank You for the deep work You have done in me. Now pour out Your Spirit on me. Light a fire on the inside of me, and fill all those places that were consumed with worry, stress, overwhelm and fear. Fill them with fresh hope and anticipation for my future. In Jesus' name. Amen.

15

Say Hello to All God Has for You

CHANGE IS BEAUTIFUL, and while it may feel impossible, it is not. You can do this, my friend. You have already shattered walls, and now you can continue to move forward one step at a time, applying the lessons you are learning though the journey. Each misstep presents an opportunity. The question is not *Can I learn?* but *Will I learn?*

We have already seen that you are on the Potter's wheel, being shaped and molded every day of your life. Simply remain on the wheel. Don't resist the process. You have said goodbye to what holds you back; now say hello to walking it out, day by day, hand in hand with Jesus. He is always there to help you and pick you up when you fall.

The walls, mindsets and lies we hear from the enemy have the power to hold us back only if we allow them to. That is the tricky part, isn't it? They seem so real and intimidating that we sometimes find it difficult to discern if there is any merit to them. In the spirit of remaining teachable, we often give those mindsets a second thought, and then a third, and a fourth, and then—uh-oh, they stick! And they become the lens through which we view ourselves. Our identity becomes "Hi, my name is Loneliness" or "I'm So Afraid" or "Insecure" or "Less Than." You see what I am saying.

But friend, as we have journeyed through the pages of this book, we have learned much about ourselves and what God says about us. We have heard the walls shatter and the resounding voice of God declaring over us, *You are My beloved daughter. You are who I say you are. And I say you are Mine.*

Yes, we are His. We are a treasure, paid for with the life of His Son. And as we grow, we learn to love God with all our hearts, minds, souls and strength, and to love our neighbors as we love ourselves. This is where we are going as sisters. We are on a "value journey," walking away from the lies of the enemy that would call us anything less than God's beautiful, chosen and much-loved daughters.

Moving Forward

I will never forget visiting my dad in his home office when I was a little girl as he worked on his doctoral dissertation, in preparation for a career in mental health. A plaque hung on the wall before him: "Study to show thyself approved unto God" (2 Timothy 2:15 KJV). But even if Dad's door was shut and he was studying, he would welcome a visit from his daughter. No matter how busy he was, he always made me feel welcome. I know this is not the case for everyone, so I do not take it lightly. I am thankful for having such an incredible, God-fearing, Jesus-loving father.

Fresh into retirement, Dad decided it was time for him to launch his ministry. He has had a call on his life for . . . well, forever. But while he was able to minister to many throughout his career as a psychologist, he experienced limits as to how much ministry he was able to offer due to restrictions governing his professional license. Still, his advice carried weight, anointing and transformation power, whether he was able to mention Jesus to people or not. That is the power of the Gospel; it flows through us to bring life to people as we declare the truth to them.

Now doors began opening for him to speak, do radio interviews, write, and more. But he, too, has experienced those mindsets that can hold us back.

Recently he was contacted about speaking at a large men's conference. I was excited for him to take that next step forward in ministry. But I should not have been surprised when he shared with me some of the initial thoughts that came to his mind.

"Krissy," he said, "immediately I heard that little lie: *You don't really want to do this. Think about all the preparation. You're retired. Stay retired.*

Wow. That label *Stay Retired*—think about that! The enemy was trying to put an identity on my dad of "Hi, my name is Retired"—whereas God was saying, *You are My son. You are called to preach the Gospel and set the captives free.*

Dad told me that God reminded him that God's own Word and His will never retire! He shared this with me to encourage me. He is fully aware of the enemy's tactics, so he moved forward with the necessary next step to respond to the invitation, in simple obedience, regardless of how he was feeling in the moment.

That is the thing with these lies—they can make us feel they might be true. A lie that says, "You're less than . . ." carries with it a sense that I *am* less than. Friend, I feel this way all the time, but like my dad, I simply move forward anyway. What ends up occurring is that the sense of being less than falls off me and I feel the strength of Champion Jesus on the inside of me, reminding me that I am more than a conquerer with and through Him. I am a warrior daughter, and I am strong in the Lord.

> In all these things we are more than conquerors through him who loved us.
>
> Romans 8:37

> He who is in you is greater than he who is in the world.
>
> 1 John 4:4 NKJV

The one in the world, the devil, whispers into your ear from the outside trying to get in. If he can lie to you by what you hear, and you listen, that lie is transferred into your thought life, which, as we have discussed, can become a mindset that you believe and then identify with. It trickles into your heart and then becomes your lens for viewing the world and yourself through. Suddenly you look into the mirror and see that defeating label, "Hi, my name is Less Than," staring back at you.

Well, enough is enough, isn't it?—because we are moving forward, full of faith, in simple obedience. We watch as those labels fall off us and the labels of *Champion, Warrior, Daughter, Friend* appear in their place.

The key, friend, is walking, progressing, moving forward, regardless of our emotions.

Walking It Out

It is important, as you are walking out who God says you are, that you extend yourself grace during the process. You have struggled with these mindsets for a long time. But there are very practical tools Jesus gives us as we are walking it out:

1. Declare Scripture over yourself.
2. Practice repetition of healthier thought patterns—what God really says about you.
3. Be patient and gracious with yourself.

All righty, now for the fun part. You have heard me mention my dad, Dr. James Torkildson, throughout the pages of this book. Now I have asked him to share with you the same advice he has given me each step of the way as I have battled these mindsets. It is advice I treasure—advice I carry with me and aim to apply each and every time an unhealthy or anti-biblical thought comes to my mind.

The advice that follows reads like one of our phone conversations. When I share with him whatever issue I am facing, he opens by reminding me who I am and the big picture overview of what is going on. Then we go into the nitty gritty and tackle it so I can keep moving forward.

Enjoy his answers to four key questions.

Advice from Dr. T.

Always remember that "if God is for us, who can be against us?" (Romans 8:31). God has a plan and call on your life. Satan wants to do all he can to sidetrack, derail and destroy you. Keeping you from God's plan is his goal. If he cannot destroy you, he will do all he can to discourage you.

Remember how he tempted Jesus in his attempt to keep Jesus from fulfilling His purpose. Satan even quoted truth to Him in an effort to derail His intention and focus. If he could get Jesus to compromise, perhaps He would not fulfill the Father's plan.

As Krissy shared earlier, after I received a call to speak at an upcoming men's conference, almost immediately the enemy whispered in my ear: *That's a lot of work. That's a lot of driv-ing to get there. Someone else can do it. You're retired. It's time to take it easy and enjoy the slow pace. You do enough already.* I knew the voice and turned my face to the Father to hear from Him.

The Lord reminded me clearly that His Word and His will do not retire. "God's gifts and his call are irrevocable" (Romans 11:29). He does not withdraw what He has given. And He uses and calls whom He chooses. As we reflect on biblical history, we see God calling His children from all walks of life to further His Kingdom and bring salvation. You are one of those whom He has called!

Remember, too, that we do not act according to emotion; we act in obedience. God does shower His love and peace on us, and the Holy Spirit certainly provides guidance, joy and comfort. However, there are and will be times when we just don't feel like doing what He has called us to do. It is then that we choose to walk in faith and obedience. We may not want to walk down the path in front of us. Many times our emotions or lack of motivation can keep us from our walk. But it is then that we say to our legs, "Walk," and when we do so, we will find ourselves on the other side, having com-pleted the task.

My advice: Walk on anyway, and you will complete the task. In that the Father will be well pleased, as He takes delight in blessing His children. God's love for you is eternal!

Ask Dr. T.[8]

1. What do I do when I am really tired and feel I just cannot overcome the lies I am hearing?

8. All advice given verbally from my dad, James Torkildson, Ed.D., www.drtletstalk.com.

Dr. T.: Take a break. This is when we need to wait upon and rest in the Lord to allow Him to renew our strength (see Isaiah 40:31). God knows we will run out of emotional or physical energy at times, which is why He has made provision for our renewal, both spiritually and physically.

2. **How do I discern the difference between reaching a limit and God's desire to stretch me in an area?**

    Dr. T.: We need to be aware of our capacity and our limits. God wants to stretch us and grow us but not break us. High stress levels can lead to distress, which in turn can lead to overwhelm, anxiety and even depression. So, yes, the Lord wants to stretch us, as this causes growth, but He has also promised not to give us more than we can handle. Often, on our own doing, we will commit to or take on more than we should. So know your limits, pray for a clear understanding of God's plan and expectations for you, and remember that His peace will remain with you as you remain in Him.

3. **What if I have made a commitment to someone, yet feel I have taken on too much and need to pull back? What is the best way to communicate to the person or people that I need to take a step back?**

    Dr. T.: This is a really good question. Here is an example of how you can approach the individual and honor him or her *and* the direction you are hearing from the Lord: "Honestly, Sally, I owe you an apology. When I said I would do this, I meant it, and had every intention of honoring the commitment. But I find I am not able to handle everything on my plate right now, and I wish I had prayed more about this before I said I would do it. I really hope you understand and that you will forgive me. I also hope this doesn't create too much of an inconvenience for you."

Most individuals will understand and accept graciously. If not, you will have to be okay with that. It is important to offer an apology and acknowledge ownership for the inconvenience, but at the end of the day, you are *not* responsible for how others feel about the choices you make. You are responsible only for doing the right thing and for doing what the Father is leading you to do. There may be times when this means a course correction.

4. I have become used to overthinking just about everything in my life. What is one of the most practical actions I can take to stop this pattern?

Dr. T.: We overthink because we don't want to be wrong or make a mistake. First, remember it is okay to do either one—be wrong or make a mistake. We are flawed; we need the Lord. "All have sinned and fall short" (Romans 3:23). We are human and it is okay.

Second, although we are called to do our best, to run the race to win (see 1 Corinthians 9:24) and to fulfill the call God has on us, we are to do so at what I call a "peace pace," which Krissy has mentioned. If we are stressed out, overthinking, worrying or multitasking to the point of experiencing anxiety, we are overworking and likely overthinking.

When you find yourself unsure or overthinking, take a break, walk away and let it go. Say to the Father, "I am taking a break and trusting You. I will move forward in faith and obedience without overthinking this." When you return to the task at hand, you will have a clearer mindset and be ready to resolve it. The results will be what they are—most often acceptable and even potentially wonderful.

Sometimes they won't be, however, and that is okay as well. Why? Because no matter how much time you spend thinking and or worrying, the results will vary and you need to not get stuck either overthinking or worrying. We make mistakes. We will until the day the Lord takes us home. And that is okay. Say it with me: "That is okay!" Simply relax and rest in the Lord and do the best you can. The Father's grace is sufficient for you, and He loves you more than you can humanly fathom.

Say Hello

Okay, me again! Thank you, Dad.

Friend, I pray this book has been a blessing to you. There is much inside you that the Lord is calling forth for this season. The time for you is right now. Are you convinced? Spend time in prayer, seeking the Lord on next steps.

And please, reach out to me. (My website is in my bio on page 191.) We are on this journey together. My goal is to create resources to empower women to be all they can be for Jesus. It would be my honor to be part of your journey in saying goodbye to what holds you back, and hello to all that God has for you.

With fresh perspective, you can see that the path before you is paved by your forerunner, King Jesus. He is there, motioning you forward into your bright future. You are stronger than you think, more capable than you know and most certainly created for the impossible. God knows you can do what He has called you to. The time is now. Let's go!

My Prayer for You

Father, thank You for my amazing new friend and the journey she has been on to shatter the walls surrounding her. Grant her peace as she moves forward in freedom. Guide her each and every step of the way. Cover her with Your shield of protection as she partners with You, believing what You say about her, and responds to Your call. In Jesus' name. Amen.

My friend, it is time to say hello to all that God has for you as you move forward in freedom through Jesus. You did it!

Krissy Nelson has a vision for you to see yourself the way God sees you. She carries a passion to release life and hope into your heart so you can walk in all that you were created for.

Krissy is a published author, life coach, speaker and TV show host who uses media as an outlet to reach the nations for Christ.

The greatest fruit of Krissy's life is found at her home on the beautiful Eastern Shore of Alabama, with her husband and their two treasured children.

For resources or booking information, visit krissynelson.com.